FRIEDRICH ENGELS

FRITZ NOVA

FRIEDRICH ENGELS:

His Contributions to

Political Theory

PHILOSOPHICAL LIBRARY
New York

For my sister Vera

CONTENTS

PREFACE

The purpose of this study is to gather, to interpret and, as far as possible, to appraise Friedrich Engels' contributions to the theories of scientific socialism, and to determine whether or not injustice has been done him in the past by lowering him to the position of junior member in a partnership with Karl Marx.

It is not the intention of this study to propose that next to Marxism a place should be cleared for "Engels-ism." The number of "isms" in political science seems to me already superabundant.

It *is* the intention of this study to establish the extent of Engels' original and positive contribution to political theory, aside from his known role as collaborator with Marx, and to examine more critically even that role.

All available references for this study have been taken directly from the German sources, and the unavoidably large quantity of footnotes, it is hoped, will speak for the reliability of the study itself. Surprisingly, little of Engels' work has been available in English; nor are extensive studies on his life and work available in many languages other than German. This posed the problem for the writer either of quoting from the German sources or of translating the given passages for the reader's convenience. The latter course was chosen; hence, most passages quoted in English but referring to German sources are my own translations.

It should also be pointed out that there exists, particularly in the English language, a critical and unpardonable shortage of studies on the life and work of Friedrich Engels. It should be a great satisfaction to this writer if, as a result of his contribution to the knowledge on this subject, further scholarly works on Engels would be forthcoming.

This study would have been impossible without the editorial assistance which it received from Mrs. Lillian Makatura Gottsegen, to whom my warmest gratitude is hereby expressed.

INTRODUCTION

It does not lie within the scope of this study to probe in any length into the intellectual influences to which Friedrich Engels may have been exposed, consciously or unconsciously, however important such an approach may be for the fullest understanding of the political concepts of Engels. Only a few remarks may here suffice. As will be seen, the plausible thesis can be defended that much in the young Engels may have been a reaction to the severe pietism which prevailed in the Duchy of Berg in general, and to the orthodox, patriarchic, upper-class atmosphere in Engels' home in particular.

It seems most profitable to limit ourselves to the major literary and socio-political influences to which young Engels was exposed. The most important prevailing literary trend in his times was called the Young German Movement. It rose out of the destruction, imbalance and uncertainty which most of Europe experienced in the wake of the French Revolution. The conservative foundation of the German monarchist absolutism was deeply affected by it for some time, i.e., during the War of Liberation against Napoleon, 1812-1813, when a number of German kings and princes promised their subjects to introduce a popular representative system and other forms of constitutionality. In the case of Prussia such promises were not kept, with far-reaching consequences for the relationship between rulers and the people, as well as for the larger problem of German national unification. The Young German Movement responded largely as opposition to the conservative era which, after the Napoleonic Wars, came to most of Europe and was commonly referred to as the Age of Metternich, and as a result of which German demands for national unification were denied by a system which, since the Congress of

Vienna, had tried to sustain itself by a policy of consistent denial of constitutionalism, democracy, liberalism and nationalism. Metternich's plan to suppress these demands and to retain for Austria the position of a pivotal state in a balance of powers encountered a growing resistance in various parts of Europe and caused a continued growth of German national liberalism. German university students formed *Burschenschaften,* whose meetings and actions became rallying points of nationalism and political liberalism.The Greek rebellion of 1829 against their Turkish overlords —one of the first major breaches in Metternich's system—evoked great enthusiasm among all those who claimed a right to a united and free Germany. Similar repercussions resulted from movements in the Netherlands, Spain, Italy and South America, and broke forth in the German (and Europe-wide) counterpart to the French Revolution in July, 1830.

In literature a similar spirit of progressivism, activism and realism was classified as "Young Germany," characterized by the opposition of its adherents to classicism and romanticism. What most of the otherwise heterogeneous groups and individuals of the Young German Movement held in common was their demand that literature must associate itself with public life and the political problems of the day, that it must absorb the problems of this world rather than romantically seek sublimations in the classical past, living in a world of suppositions, medievalism and artificiality.

The two most representative exponents of the Young German Movement, however debatable this classification may seem, were Ludwig Boerne and Heinrich Heine.

Boerne (1784-1834) was primarily a political journalist whose first publications appeared in his journals, the *Zeitschwingen* (1817) and the *Wage* (1821), thereafter in Cotta's *Morgenblatt.* In order to avoid the censorship of his political polemics, he disguised his attacks skillfully under the cloak of criticism of fine arts, literature, musical and societal events. After the July, 1830, Revolution, Boerne took his residence in Paris and moved increasingly from liberalism to radical republicanism. Although his greatest merit consisted perhaps in contemporary polemics, Boerne may be said to have exercised considerable influence on contemporary literature by his informal journalistic yet spirited style.[1] As Engels wrote, under the pseudonym of "Friedrich Oswald," in his "Vorlesungen ueber die moderne Literatur der Deutschen," published in the *Deutsche Jahrbuecher fuer Wissenschaft und Kunst,* June 15, 1842, Boerne should be considered the practical counterpart of the theoretical Hegel, whom Boerne implemented significantly. According to Engels, Boerne was a man of "iron personality," of "impressive firmness of will," "unique in German history," the "banner-carrier of German freedom," in brief, "the only *man* in Germany of his time."

In his earlier poetry Heinrich Heine (1797-1856) impresses the reader as starkly sentimental-romantic, rich in imagination and gifted with subtle irony. His literary fame began later with his *Harzreise* and *Reisebilder* (1826), which seemed to appeal to many of his readers because of the penetrating witticism and cynicism he applied to many of his contemporary conditions. Shortly after the French Revolution of 1830, Heine decided to move to Paris, asserting that "freedom was the religion of our time" and that the French were the chosen people of that new religion. Though one may count Heine among the most lyrical of German poets, he frequently impressed or perhaps disturbed his readers when the lyrical, idyllic poetry seemed suddenly destroyed or satirically perverted by the additions of biting dissonance, probably the result of the pessimism and adverse experiences of his own life. Besides being a poet, Heinrich Heine was also an accomplished political journalist, in fact one of the first great modern critical and literary feuilletonists of Europe. Heine also foresaw the growing tension in German-French relations, the coming of a major world war, the concept of a world government and social revolution. Engels wrote in *The New Moral World,* Nr. 25, December 13, 1844, that Heine was "the most outstanding (*Hervorragenste*) among all living German poets," who was also the author of political lyric and had announced (*angekuendigt*) the advent of socialism. He had joined (*sich uns angeschlossen*) "the most active literary personalities among the German socialists." [2]

Heine's influence on socialists such as Engels consisted in his realistic and progressive views, his breaking away from romanticism, his battle against political reactionism, his rejection of exaggerated nationalism, and his strong support of the emancipation of all peoples. There are many references in Heine which indicate his general indifference to religion and a probable infatuation with Saint Simonism. His *Zur Geschichte der Philosophie in Deutschland,* written in 1834, indicate that, similarly to Engels, Heine went through a period of political idealism and natural philosophy before he arrived at revolutionary republicanism. In fact, Heine stated unmistakably that the road to revolution led through philosophy.

The following serves as a keen summary of Heine's particular importance for nineteenth-century German literature:

Heine possesses the fullest freedom of an artist in the means of expression which were furnished by German romanticism, and uses them far more methodically. At the same time, he represents more and more the materialist world-sentiment which, in contrast to the romantic period, began to burst through by 1830. His political radicalism turned also against the confession of faith of the later romanticism. He fights for freedom in the spirit of the French Revolution. With him and through him German poetry declares itself in favor of overthrow (*Umsturzlust*).[3]

Of major influence, particularly for the academic circles of the progressive national movement, became the teachings of Hegel whose lectures in the University of Berlin, especially on the philosophy of law, appealed to his listeners as he steered between the theory of the social contract and the theory of the organic state (Karl von Rotteck versus Karl Ludwig von Haller) toward the notion of the state as the realization of the highest ethical fulfillment of man. After Hegel's death in 1831, a number of divisions occurred among his followers, which was not too astounding in view of the incompatibility of schools of thought (such as the state absolutists and liberals) which all claimed their origin in Hegel's teachings. The growing intellectual schism was particularly evident in the field of religious philosophy, which commenced during Hegel's lifetime in his disagreement with Immanuel Kant and Friedrich Schleiermacher. It was a disciple of Hegel himself, David Friedrich Strauss, whose book on the *Leben Jesu* (1835) ushered in a number of critical, although erudite, theological investigations questioning the credibility of New Testament scriptures. Leaders among these authors were Ferdinand Christian Bauer, Ludwig Feuerbach and Bruno Bauer. The ensuing controversy centered between conservative Hegelians and liberal Young Hegelians, the former rejecting and the latter approving Strauss' book on the *Life of Christ*.[4]

The intellectual controversy was not limited to theology alone. In fact, hardly any field of knowledge escaped a similar division into liberal and orthodox-conservative schools of thought, adopting or rejecting the new, critical and realistic approach. Thus in the classics, the older culture- and history-oriented approach represented by Otfried Mueller, Karl Theodor Welcker and others faced a more critical, grammar-conscious approach expounded by Gottfried Hermann. In historiography, the romantic school, such as Friedrich Raumer's, was challenged by the critical methodology of Friedrich Christoph Dahlmann and Leopold Ranke. The natural philosophy of Friedrich Wilhelm Schelling, Henrik Steffens and Gotthilf Heinrich von Schubert, met the opposition of new mathematicians and physicists such as Georg Simon Ohm, Wilhelm Weber and Karl Friedrich Gauss. In poetry Georg Gottfried von Gervinus introduced new methods into the study of poetry. In technology, the first railway was operated in Germany between the cities of Nuremberg and Fuerth on December 7, 1835. Such outstanding economists as Friedrich List and Paul Pfizer pointed out the economic advantages that would accrue to Germany if national political unity were obtained. In general, industry and agriculture moved rapidly ahead.

BIOGRAPHICAL INTRODUCTION

Friedrich Engels, son of a textile manufacturer after whom he was named and of Elizabeth Francisca Mauritzia, née Van Haar, was born in Barmen in the Wuppertal on November 28, 1820. His homeland in the Prussian Rhine Province was at that time the most industrialized territory of Germany, one in which the young Engels could study at first-hand the development and effects of the newly rising capitalist industrial society with its concurrent clashes between labor and management. In his own descriptions of his youth in 1839, Engels indicated his first awareness of social problems ("social injustices," from his point of view) and his concern for the worsening conditions of the working class. These include the poverty prevailing among many of the workers, craftsmen and small businessmen in Barmen and Elberfeld, the frequent use of child labor in the factories, the unsanitary and hazardous conditions of all factory workers, the lack of effective management on the part of the owners, the fierce competition of the industries among themselves, and the long hours of labor for factory workers as well as for those who still worked at the looms in their own homes.[1] He takes notice also in his earliest observations of the pietistic movement of Protestantism (to which he objected) and the presence of cheap brandy (*Bibel und Schnaps*), for Engels the only two available outlets for the depressed workers.[2]

It was in this environment that Engels was raised, although his own family belonged to the well-to-do. His father was described as a domineering, intolerant, possessive patriarch. As Gustav Mayer wrote in the only existing comprehensive biography of Engels, *Friedrich Engels: Eine Biographie,* Friedrich Engels' parents were quite concerned about their fifteen-year-old son. In a letter to his wife, the elder Engels expressed concerned over

Friedrich's mediocre grades in school, as well as his lack of obedience in spite of the stress on discipline at home. The letter also referred to the "disquieting lack of thoughtfulness and of character" which Friedrich displayed, although the same letter recognized his "other pleasant qualities."[3] These remarks may very well establish a fatherly concern about Friedrich's first symptoms of rebellion against society. It is of some interest to observe also that Friedrich was unable to complete his secondary gymnasium education and hence was not qualified to attend the university. Unlike the education of Karl Marx, that of Engels was, therefore, considerably less advanced and, as it were, incomplete.

Since Marx in many economic crises during his life was saved only by the generosity of Engels, it is necessary to mention that against the latter's own preference and inclination his father forced him to become a businessman. In this capacity, however, he was able to travel extensively and thus broaden his intellectual horizons, and at the same time (fortunately for Marx) to attain sufficient financial solvency.

To round out this brief biographical introduction I should mention, also, Engels' general intellectual alertness, his many interests, his ability to make friends, his gifts of observation, and, finally, his love of sports and physical exercise.

Engels' initiation into the company of the prominent representatives of modern socialism began in 1844 when his "Outlines for a Critique of National Economy" ("Umrisse zu einer Kritik der Nationaloekonomie") first appeared in the *Deutsch-Franzoesische Jahrbuecher,* edited by Marx and Arnold Ruge.[4] In these sketches some of the more general, though not yet fully developed, principles of scientific socialism were contained.

Engels had met Marx for the first time and briefly at the offices of the *Rheinische Zeitung* in Cologne in November, 1842, and later began his correspondence with Marx in early 1844 in connection with the publication of his essay "Outlines for a Critique of National Economy." Their meeting in Paris at the end of August, 1844, however, marked the beginning of a more serious collaboration and agreement on principles between the two men.

In 1845 Engels published "The Position of the Working Class in England" ("Die Lage der arbeitenden Klasse in England") in Manchester, where he then resided.[5] It was a significant work, as Marx himself stated on May 5, 1880, in his preface to the French edition of Engels' "The Development of Socialism from Utopia to Science" ("Die Entwicklung des Sozialismus von der Utopie zur Wissenschaft").[6]

During his stay in England and later in Brussels, Engels was a contributor to the *Northern Star,* the official organ of the socialist movement, and to the *New Moral World* of Robert Owen. During his residence in Brussels, Engels founded, with Marx, the Communist German Labor Association, an organization connected with Flemish and Walloon associations. Marx and Engels also became co-editors of the *German-Brussels Zeitung.* Both became members of the German committee of the League of the Just in London, the precursor of the International League of Communists (*Bund der Kommunisten*). In 1847 at the International Congress of the League in London, Marx and Engels were assigned to draft the Communist Manifesto, which was published shortly before the French Revolution of 1848. After this February Revolution Engels was made one of the editors of the *Neuen Rheinischen Zeitung,* originally founded by Marx in Cologne in 1848 and suppressed in May, 1849, against Prussia.

In 1850 Engels became a collaborator with Marx in the *Neuen Rheinischen Zeitung*: *Politisch-Oekonomische Revue* in London. In this journal Engels published for the first time his article "The German Peasants' War" ("Der deutsche Bauernkrieg"), which was reprinted as a brochure in Leipzig nineteen years later and reached three editions. In the 'fifties Engels wrote many articles for such socialist papers as *Volksstaat* and *Vorwaerts,* most of them being reprinted later in pamphlet form. Typical of this group are articles such as these: "Social Reports from Russia" ("Soziales aus Russland"), "Prussian Liquor in the German Parliament" ("Preussischer Schnaps im deutschen Reichstag"), "On the Problem of Housing" ("Zur Wohnungsfrage"), and "The Bakunists at Work" ("Die Bakunisten an der Arbeit"). After Engels had moved from Manchester to London in 1870 he became a member of the General Council of the International, in which capacity he handled all correspondence with Spain, Portugal and Italy. In 1878 he wrote the important "Anti-Duehring: Herr Eugen Duehring's Revolution," ("Herrn Eugen Duehrings Umwaelzung der Wissenschaft"), designed to be a reply to Professor Duehring's theories of socialism. These appeared first as a series of articles in the *Vorwaerts* and later in book form, and represented an introduction to scientific socialism.

In the twelve years in which he survived Marx (1883-1895), Engels wrote in addition to many other articles, "The Origin of the Family, Private Property and the State" ("Der Ursprung der Familie, des Privateigentums und des Staats"). This appeared in 1884 and was a significant contribution to the socialist theory of the state, as well as a valuable elaboration of the materialist conception of history. Another work belonging to that period was "Ludwig Feuerbach and the Outcome of Classical German Philosophy" ("Ludwig Feuerbach und der Ausgang der klassischen deutschen Philosophie"), first published in the *Neue Zeit* in 1886. It dealt with Hegelian ideological philosophy and with Feuerbach's conception of materialism. In the 1890's Engels wrote significant letters to such contemporary socialists as Paul Ernst, Joseph Block and Franz Mehring, in which he explored once more the theory of historical materialism. Most of this time, however, he devoted to working on the completion of the second, third and fourth volumes of Marx's *Das Kapital*. Lenin's remark is appropriate here: that after Marx's death it was Engels alone who continued to be the "counselor and leader" of the European socialists. "They all drew from the rich treasury of the knowledge and experience of the old Engels." [7]

Other targets which Engels singled out for attack were the reformists and ultra-revolutionaries, the British Fabians and other "sentimental socialists and philanthropists," the anarchists, and a long list of "objectionable" individuals, groups and organizations which Engels had designated as "opportunists." At the occasion of the Erfurt Party Convention of the Social Democrats in 1891, Engels still took an active part in the criticism of the theoretical portion of the Erfurt Program, expressing his doubts about the feasibility of a peaceful accomplishment of socialism.[8]

The last work of Engels was the "Introduction" to the "Class Struggles in France" ("Einleitung" to the "Klassenkaempfen in Frankreich"), 1848-1850, which was drafted in London between February 14 and March 6, 1895, under the impact of further anti-socialist legislation in Germany. Engels advised the proletarians to utilize all legal means to prepare the proletariat for the socialist revolution.[9]

Engels died of cancer on August 5, 1895. His body was cremated and his ashes scattered into the ocean along the coast of Eastbourne, according to his own instructions.

FRIEDRICH ENGELS

CHAPTER I

SOCIAL THEORY: TO CONDEMN OR CONDONE?

Engels repeatedly indicated that he recognized the need for a social theory. When he referred to the progress of "philosophical communism" in Germany (in the same article in which he had mentioned Marx for the first time), he wrote:

Germans have a philosophical nature and do not want to and cannot give up communism as long as it is founded on sound philosophical principles . . . The same love of abstract principle, the same disregard for reality and self-interest which have brought the Germans into a condition of political insignificance, precisely these same qualities guarantee the success of philosophical communism in this country.[10]

Similarly, in articles on the utopian socialist Charles Fourier, Engels mocked the Germans as these "erudite gentlemen" who were sailing hither and yon in "bottomless" theory in order to fish for the "principle" of socialism.[11]

Again, in discussing Hegel's ideological approach to the philosophy of history which, according to Engels, placed the realm of religious fantasy over and above the realities of life, Engels wrote that the Germans should rid themselves of their senseless theoretical phrases and at last come to realize that they must search for the causes of problems in *actually existing* and changing conditions.[12]

Commenting on Marx's *A Critique of Political Economy* (*Zur Kritik der Politischen Oekonomie*) in defense of the Marxian "revolutionary discovery" that the modes of production of material life condition all social, political and intellectual processes, Engels alleged that this new concept was simple enough

1

to be understood by everybody who was not befuddled by "idealistic hocus-pocus." History, politics and patriotism should be conceived, Engels wrote, in terms of materialism and should not be interpreted by the "magic formulae," of *liberté, égalité, fraternité,* which the Germans so glibly plagiarized from the French.[13]

Similarly, Engels argued against Proudhon's tendency to measure all things by an idealized concept of *justice éternelle.* In place of a non-existent eternal justice, the product of Proudhon's "economic ignorance and helplessness," Engels postulated the iron rule of economic laws.[14] Men must not forget, he advised, the origin of their social laws in the economic conditions of life, just as the laws of man's physical existence had their origin in the animal kingdom. "Justice" is but the idealized, mystically adored expression of existing economic circumstances. There were different concepts of right and wrong, different approaches to questions of justice, and differing evaluations of what is right for Greeks and Romans, as these were applied to feudalism, the bourgeoisie and even the Prussian Junker.[15] Engels contrasted the deterministic, concrete approach taken in Marx's *Das Kapital,* which was not abstract, formalized socialism, but the result of twenty-five years of empirical work and self-criticism, with the "wonder-cures for all social ills, the ready-made social plan of salvation, the system of Proudhon."[16]

These practical proposals for the elimination of all social evils, these social universal cures, have always and everywhere been the makeshift products of founders of sects who appeared at a time when the proletarian movement was still in its swaddling clothes . . . The development of the proletarian . . . causes these swaddling clothes to be cast aside as outgrown and makes the workers' class understand that nothing is more impractical than the previously excogitated 'practical solution' adaptable to all cases; and that practical socialism consists rather in the right recognition of the capitalist modes of production in all their respects.[17]

When Eugen Duehring of the University of Berlin announced his conversion to socialism in 1875, he presented to his German audience what Engels called a "complicated" socialist theory, in addition to a practical plan for the reorganization of society. In so doing Duehring rejected, among other things, Marx's brand of socialism. Engels undertook the attack on Duehring in a series of articles which first appeared in the Leipzig *Vorwaerts* in 1877 and 1878 and were later published, revised and in book form, in Zurich in the year 1886. In his preface to the English edition of 1892 Engels criticized Duehring by commenting on the proverbial German tendency to profoundness and thoroughness which seemed to compel anybody who came out with a new proposition to enlarge it into an elaborate all-encompassing theoretical system:

> He has to prove that the first principles of logic as well as the fundamental laws of the universe had existed from all eternity for no other purpose than to lead, in the last instance, to the crowning of this newly discovered theory. And in this respect Dr. Duehring fits perfectly into the national pattern.[18]

Nonetheless, Engels was himself too much the product of the German school of theory to condemn uncompromisingly all impact of theory on socialism. He was ready to admit that, after all, theory had a definite claim and place in the history of socialism. Thus he alleged that the German workers had a double advantage over those of the rest of Europe, first because they belonged to Europe's "most theoretical" people and secondly because they had preserved their "theoretical sense." Without the precedent of German philosophy, particularly that of Hegel, German scientific socialism—the only scientific socialism that had ever existed—would never have come into existence. "Without a theoretical sense among the workers scientific socialism would never have passed into their flesh and blood, as is the case." Engels singled out indifference to all theory as the chief deterrent to progress in the British labor movement; Proudhonism was the chief cause of confusion among the French and Belgians; and Bakunism was the chief culprit among the Spanish and Italian workers.[19] He reasoned that strength of the German workers' movement consisted, in the ability to combat capitalism theoretically, as well as politically. The scientific socialist leader, precisely because socialism had become scientific, was obliged to become well versed in all the theories underlying theoretical socialism.[20]

We may gain some insight into Engel's apparently inconsistent attitude concerning the value of theory by examining his statement in "The Development of Socialism from Utopia to Science" that the theories of modern socialism seemed initially to be a consistent continuation of the French Enlightenment of the eighteenth century and in fact *had* to link themselves, like all other new theories, to the existing ideological stock, "although their roots (ultimately) rested in materialistic economic facts."[21] In the last analysis, Engels alleged in another statement, all social philosophy was highly *incomplete*. Hegel's method should be applied, suggested Engels, by setting up a premise for further evolutionary development, rather than considering thoughts "fixed" for all times.[22] No rigidly opposite poles existed, Engels explained in a letter to Franz Mehring on July 14, 1893, between a completely ideological and completely materialist approach. Marx and he preferred to place the *main* emphasis on the basis of economic facts, deriving political, juridical and ideological notions from them. This did not preclude a total disregarding of any interaction: "Once a historical element has been brought into the world by other elements, ultimately by economic facts, it also reacts in its turn and may react on its environment and even on its own causes."[23] Engels only condemned a one-sided approach in which the ideologist "imagined false or apparent motives," believing that because his ideology was a pure process of thought he derived both its form and its contents from pure thought. Working with "mere thought material," the ideologist accepted it "without examining it as the product of thought."[24]

Conceding to theory its proper place in the development of the history of man, provided that its primary socio-economic rootedness was never left out of sight, Engels was himself able to formulate a theory which, by turning against Hegel's ideologized philosophy, established (with Marx) socialist dialectics and through its application to history the concept of economic determinism or materialism. Socialist dialectics, as conceived by Engels, was in essence a substitution of materialist philosophy or *Real-*

Philosophie, to borrow the German political term, for Hegel's classical idealism. The dialectic role of philosophy as an end in itself was to be taken over by dialectics as a theory and method applied to history and the natural sciences. In this substitution Engels did not deny some recognition of Hegel's achievements, and he called Hegel's *History of Philosophy*, even in later years, "one of the most ingenious works of all times." Engels was particularly indebted to Hegel's dialectics, the "science of interrelationship and motion." As he wrote in "The Development of Socialism," "the newer German philosophy . . . found its completion in Hegel."[25] For Engels, Hegel's philosophy had its greatest merit in the reestablishing of dialectics as the "highest form of thinking." Essentially it was a return to Greek dialectics and most particularly to that of Aristotle, who had already explored its most important forms and applications.

Later dialectic philosophy, argued Engels, although it produced such outstanding men as Descartes, Spinoza, Diderot and Rousseau, had lost its original strength by the eighteenth century when it had become bogged down in metaphysics. The essence of dialectic thinking for Engels was to explain nature, the history of mankind and human thinking in terms of "infinite mazes of interrelationships and reciprocal effects in which nothing remains constant but all moves, changes, rises and perishes."[26] None had pronounced this more clearly than the Greek philosopher Heraclitus with his dictum that "all is in a flow and in continuous change." But in striving for an explanation of the totality of existence, Engels felt that the Greeks had failed to discover the details which composed the totality. This became a task for post-Grecian natural scientists and historians who, after compiling the data were able to systematize, compare and categorize them. But in this process, these philosophers had lost sight of the totality in the cobweb of the components, which led to stagnation in place of progressive motion. The outcome of this tendency, highlighted in Bacon and Locke, became metaphysical ideology. Its characteristics were to look at things, thoughts and concepts as separate, rigid, static, absolute phenomena.[27] In its quest for the statics, metaphysical ideology had lost sight of existing contradictions and conflicts, of origin and ending.

Dialectics, however, as Engels described it, recognized poles of contrast which, whether positive or negative, were nonetheless inseparable from each other and organically interwoven in spite of contrast. It conceived of the universe as one of eternal forces and counter-forces, of changes, causes and changing effects. Dialectics, he wrote, thinks of interlinked and interrelated connections, of motion, growth and decay. Nature was the great proof of the correctness of dialectics and modern natural science corroborated this; nature was essentially dialectic, not metaphysical, and could not be confined parochially.

Engels felt strongly that it was the immortal merit of Darwin to have shown that in nature, plants and animals, as well as humans, were the result of evolutionary processes occurring over millions of years. It was deplorable, argued Engels, that few natural philosophers had been able to tear themselves away from theoretical to dialectic-materialist natural science.[28] Kant, Newton and Laplace had shown the way from statics to dynamics. The apex of dialectics was then reached by Hegel, who was the first to realize that all natural, historical and intellectual matters were in a continuous process of motion, change, transformation and development, eradicating therefore all that seemed to be incidental or planless and establishing scientific laws in the process of the development of mankind.

Yet Hegel's epoch-making discovery, which made his the "most universal" brain of his time and revealed his "enormously historical sense,"[29] was lamentably diminished by the limits of his own knowledge, by the limits of knowledge and concepts of his epoch, and most of all, by the fact that he was an idealist who, instead of recognizing real things and events accepted them only as external images of some ideal reality. "Thereby everything stood on its head," Engels wrote emphatically, "and the true connection of the world completely reversed."[30] Hegel's system thus turned out to be a "colossal miscarriage" and suffered from its inner contradiction: it presupposed that the history of mankind was a process of development, rejecting therefore the notion of verifiable absolute truths; on the other hand, it came to be the very epitome of absolute truth in its claim to possession of an all-embracing, finite system of knowledge—a direct con-

6

tradiction to the very essence of dialectic thinking. As Gustav Mayer put it most appropriately in his biography of Engels, "Hegel's world-historical deed was that he pronounced the (dialectic) law for the first time and in general form; his mistake was that he developed it as a mere law of thought and imposed it upon nature and history instead of deriving it from them."[31]

While Engels turned away from Hegel's dialectic idealism, he did not fail to restate his greatness, in spite of the alleged "abstract confusion" which Hegel had introduced to the *real* philosophy of history. As Engels wrote, "The excellency of the fundamental concept is remarkable even today."[32]

Engels claimed that Marx was the only one who was able to penetrate the kernel of truly original thought in Hegel's logic by retaining the dialectic method freed from its idealistic encumbrances and molding it into the "proper" form. The result of this rescue mission, according to Engels, was Marx's *Kritik der politischen Oekonomie.*[33] According to this statement, Engels appears to give Marx all the credit. Yet we find that Engels uses the personal pronouns "we" and "they" a number of times in his discussion of how "they" (presumably Marx *and* Engels) had analyzed dialectics and, by applying it to political economy, had found that it had to be studied in terms of relationships and counter-relationships—not as abstract thought-processes, but as "real occurrences;" and in terms of clashes between theses and their antitheses.[34]

A similar statement exists in Engels' preface to the second edition of the "Anti-Duehring" of 1885, in which he wrote, "Marx and I were pretty well the only people to rescue conscious dialectics from the German idealist philosophy and to apply it to the materialist conception of nature and history."[35] In this same preface Engels asserted that it became their endeavor to strip the mysticism from Hegel's dialectics (which Hegel had developed as all-embracing but mystic form) and to bring it clearly before the mind in its complete simplicity and universality.[36]

The first and one half of the second chapter *Ludwig Feuerbach* (which study was also designed as a critical review of C. N. Starke's work *Ludwig Feuerbach,* 1885) were primarily concerned with the rejection of Hegel's philosophy of the state.[37]

According to Engels, Hegel's state had been raised to the level of a "royal Prussian philosophy," with far-reaching consequences for the cause of the German revolutionary movement of the nineteenth century: Hegel had given this world the philosophical revolutionary truth that nothing in human thought and action could be sought in the form of dogmatic absolutes but were the result of a long, historical-scientific process by which everything ascended from a lower to a higher phase which, in turn, would strive toward the next higher one. As in philosophy, so in practical life, too, no absolute, ideal condition could be reached, as Hegel had shown. Every phase was important in itself, but must give room to the next higher for which it served. For dialectic philosophy, Engels asserted, nothing was finite, absolute, or sacred. The only absolute in Hegel's philosophy was that it recognized definite stages in the dialectic development, determined by time and circumstances. Hegel failed, however, according to Engels, when he endeavored to discover ways and means of bringing the dialectic process to an end (in the search for absolute ideas), a contradiction to Hegel's entire dogmatic system indeed, although understandable for anybody who tried to construe a "system" (and a "system" must aim at an end somewhere and sometime). As a result, Engels stated, Hegel's "revolutionary" dialectics tended to become "conservative."[38] In the end, Hegel was compelled by the logics of his own theory to conceive of the petty bourgeoisie which supported the regime of the unimaginative King Frederick William III of Prussia as the final realization of the "absolute idea" of the state. Nonetheless, and in spite of its shortcomings, Engels concluded that Hegel's dialectics helped to bring about the end of philosophy, pointing the way "out of the labyrinth of systems to the real positive recognition of the world."[39] What needed to be done, Engels concluded, was to replace Hegel's *absolute ideas* with a *materialism of nature*.

But who was called to accomplish that necessary task? Ludwig Feuerbach (1804-1874), one of the leading materialist philosophers of the pre-Marxist period and an exponent of the radical bourgeois democratic ideologists?

According to Engels, Feuerbach went through a transition

from Hegelianism to materialism, in the process of which Feuerbach had to break away at some point from Hegel's idealism. In fact, Feuerbach experienced this at the moment when he came to realize that Hegel's absolute idea was nothing more than a remnant of faith in an other-worldly Creator. In its place Feuerbach advocated the theory that matter was not a product of the mind, but that the mind itself was only the highest product of matter.[40] This was "pure materialism," and Engels approved of it. But Feuerbach was unwilling to draw the further conclusion that materialism, as the foundation of all human essence and knowledge, was the foundation also of *natural science,* as well as of *social science.* Feuerbach failed to grasp the fact that materialism, like idealism, was subject to stages of development. Materialism of the eighteenth century was essentially mechanical, Engels admitted; in chemistry, biology, zoology and botany, science still operated exclusively "mechanically-minded" and was largely unaware of the existence of other, higher laws which underlay the mechanical laws.[41] Because of the limitation in that stage of materialism, it sought compensation in metaphysical, i.e., essentially anti-dialectic, philosophy. The eighteenth century was still essentially unhistorical and convinced that all phenomena were repetitious, rather than progressively ascending, evolutionary stages. The narrowness of this approach became particularly obstructive at a time when the natural sciences began to have a foreboding of great potentialities of the later theories of evolution.[42] Instead of developing the scientific progress which they experienced in the direction of progressive evolution, the eighteenth century materialists, and those of the nineteenth century, culminating in Feuerbach, took refuge in interpreting the progress in the sciences as a renewed evidence for the existence of a world Creator. Engels suggested that Feuerbach should not be blamed too much for his failure to bring into harmony societal and historico-philosophical sciences with materialism, since the full knowledge of natural science was still largely inaccessible to him.[43]

For Engels the clearest evidence of Feuerbach's contamination by Hegel's idealism, was his views on religious philosophy and ethics. According to Engels, Feuerbach interpreted and

9

sublimated religion as a sentimental relationship between men, solemnizing religiously the social and sexual relationship among men, the friendships, compassions, self-sacrifice, etc., instead of conceiving them merely as purely human relationships.[44] For Engels, pure human relationships had already degenerated by a society which was built on class antagonism. Putting them into a framework of religion enhanced this degeneration, transformed a history of class war into a mere "appendix to church history."[45] God himself was the product of a long process of abstraction, the concentrated quintessence of former polytheistic tribal and national gods. Correspondingly, man, too, supposedly the image of God, became an abstracted, i.e., idealized man, instead of a "real" being, the quintessence of many "real" beings. Feuerbach who had preached the doctrine of material nature, of the concreteness and reality, had turned to abstraction as soon as he had come to speak about the relationships of men.[46] As Engels wrote,

> Feuerbach's moral theory will experience what all their predecessors have experienced. It is tailored to all times, all peoples, all circumstances, and becomes therefore forever inapplicable. It remains powerless in face of the real world, as Kant's categoric imperative. In reality, every class, in fact, every professional group, possesses its own morality and breaks even that (morality), whenever it can do it with impunity. Love, which is supposed to unite all, turns into wars, disputes, lawsuits, domestic quarrels, divorces and most complete exploitations of men by his (so-called) fellow-men.[47]

Feuerbach failed to abandon the world of abstraction and could not find the road to the world of reality. Yet, the logical conclusion which he omitted to draw must be drawn nonetheless: The cult of the abstract man, which formed Feuerbach's core for his new religion, must be replaced by the science of the real man and his historical development.[48]

Since Feuerbach failed, the task of dissolving Hegel's school of thought devolved on Marx and himself (i.e., Engels, who asserted at that point that he had a "certain, separate (selbstaendig) share" in the elaboration of this theory).[49]

The severing from the Hegelian philosophy resulted also

10

here in the return to the materialist standpoint. That is, one decided to conceive of the real world-nature and history—as it renders itself to anybody who approaches it without preconceived idealistic moods (Schrullen). One decided to bring mercilessly to the altar every idealistic mood which could not bring its inner coherence into harmony with phantastic, conceived facts. And that is all that materialism stands for, except that here, for the first time, materialist *Weltanschauung* was taken seriously by applying it consistently to all appropriate areas of knowledge,—at least in its fundamentals. Hegel was not simply put aside: On the contrary, one tied his . . . revolutionary aspect to the dialectic method.[50]

The adherence of Hegel and other Germans to dialectic idealism led Engels to the dialectics of materialism which therefore travelled from metaphysical to "scientific" materialism. This was not accomplished, however, without some rivalry from other unexpected sources. There are passages in Engels' writings where he not only distinguished between idealism and materialism, but also between "mechanical" determinism (and evidently "non-mechanical" determinism).[51] The latter was also referred to by Engels as "undialectic abstract" materialism from which he disassociated himself as much as from the idealistic. In brief, Engels grouped together the "mechanical materialists" (*Vulgaermaterialisten*) as those who were willing to subscribe to materialism only to the degree of recognizing its impact on nature by man. This "one-sided" materialism, Engels asserted, ignored the important aspect of the reciprocity and versatility of the dialectic process.[52]

Similarly Engels, in agreement with Marx, rejected the *limited application* of the materialism of Ludwig Feuerbach. Feuerbach did not extend it to society and social institutions, and preferred rather to observe an attitude of passivity, or even to apply the "idealistic" Hegelian interpretation. Engels, conversely, asserted that the study of the human society had taught him that the social scene was a most appropriate area to which to apply the materialist analysis.

In Engels' preface to his *Ludwig Feuerbach and the End of*

11

Classical German Philosophy he stated significantly that he has not had any chance for more than forty years (while Marx was still alive) to discuss with him again the ideas expounded by Feuerbach, in spite of the fact that he (Feuerbach) "in many respects was a link between Hegelian philosophy and our concepts."[53] In view of a veritable renaissance of classical German philosophy, Engels continued, he felt obliged to devote himself to the writing of an analysis of Feuerbach's work (which the *Neue Zeit* published in 1886 and the Dietz Verlag revised and re-published in Stuttgart in 1888).

In preparation for that assignment, Engels wrote, he took reference to Marx's Eleven Theses on Feuerbach which Engels had found among Marx's notes. These were, in Engels' words, designed to be elaborated later by Marx and were swiftly jotted down in 1845, certainly "not intended by Marx to be printed [in that form]."[54]

According to Engels, Marx had completed the major features of the development of his materialist concept of history when he (Marx) wrote the theses in the spring of 1845.[55] Engels who edited them later referred to them as "the first document in which the congenial germ of the new concept of life was laid down."[56]

In the following excerpts from Marx's Theses on Feuerbach will be given, to form a point of reference to the better understanding of Engels' completion and implementation upon them:

The chief defect of all hitherto existing materialism—that of Feuerbach included—is the thing (*Gegenstand*), reality, sensuousness, is conceived only in the form of the *object* (*Objekt*) or of *contemplation* (*Anschauung*), but not as *human sensuous activity, practice,* not subjectively. Hence it happened that the *active* side, in contradistinction to materialism, was developed by idealism—but only abstractly, since, of course, idealism does not know real, sensuous activity as such . . . He (Feuerbach) does not grasp the significance of "revolutionary," of "practical-critical," activity. The question whether objective (gegenstaendliche) truth can be attributed to human thinking is not a question of theory, but is a *practical* question. In practice man must prove the truth, that is, the reality and power, the this-sided-ness (*Diesseitigkeit*) of his thinking. The dispute over the reality or non-reality of thinking which is isolated from practice is a purely *scholastic* question . . . For Feuerbach the religious essence constitutes the human essence. Yet the human essence is not an abstraction inherent in the individual. His reality constitutes the totality of social relationships . . . Feuerbach . . . is compelled to abstract from the historical process to fix (*sic*) for himself a religious spirit, and to presuppose an abstract-isolated-human individual . . . Social life is essentially *practical*. All mysteries which mislead theory to mysticism find their rational solution in human practice and in the comprehension of this practice. The highest point attained by *contemplative* materialism, that is, materialism which does not understand sensuousness as practical activity, is the contemplation of single individuals in "civil society." The standpoint of the old materialism is *civil* society; the standpoint of the new is *human* society, or socialized humanity. The philosophers have only *interpreted* the world, in various ways; the point, however, is to *change* it.

For Engels, an appraisal of Feuerbach was "a full recognition of the influence" which Feuerbach had, more than any other post-Hegelian philosopher, "upon us,"—as an unpaid "debt of honor" toward him.[57]

CHAPTER II

IDEALISM AND MATERIALISM
IN SCIENCE AND HISTORY

The most cogent explanation which Engels has offered as to why he had decided to lay the foundations of a new, modern materialist dialectics which was to become the very core of a scientific system, was that he had sensed the existence of analogies between events in the social, economic and political spheres and those in the natural sciences. Engels was evidently inspired by the major work of Darwin which he had read shortly after its publication in 1859. He had also immediately recognized the enormous bearing which Darwin's theory of the origin and development of the species would have on *all* science with the possibility of drawing parallels between the principles of natural selection and the dialectic empirical approach.[58]

Engels may have been influenced in this view by a letter from Marx on December 19, 1860, in which the latter wrote:

> During my time of trial, these last four weeks, I have read all sorts of things. Among others Darwin's book on Natural Selection. Although it is developed in the crude English style, this is the book which contains the basis in natural history for our view.[59]

According to one source, Engels is said to have stated that with Darwin's new scientific theory of the natural selection, "the old teleology had been sent to the devil." The concept of the existence of immutable biological laws had run its course, a concept which had always been in conflict with Hegel's theory of necessity and fortuitousness, or even worse with the school of mechanical determinism.[60] For Engels, Darwin's theory of selection confirmed Hegel's dialectics. He pointed out in *"The De-*

14

velopment of Socialism," etc., "that nature offered the best proof of the correctness of the dialectic approach, and not of metaphysical methods of thinking." And then he added, "in this connection Darwin must be named before all others. He dealt the metaphysical conception of nature the heaviest blow by his proof that all organic beings, plants, animals, and men themselves were the products of a process of evolution, going on over a period of millions of years."[61]

However, in a letter to the Russian socialist Peter Lavrov on November 12, 1875, Engels seemed to have qualified his acceptance of Darwin, approving his theory of development, but not fully his methods of proving it. Specifically Engels objected to his explaining all historical evolution in terms of a battle for existence. This was a particularly unsatisfactory explanation of history for Engels, who was unwilling to interpret class struggle as merely a form of Darwinian battle for existence. Engels rather expressed the idea that Darwin's theory was related to Hobbes' *bellum omnium contra omnes,* to the bourgeois economic theory of competition, and to the Malthusian theory of population.[62]

It was natural science, as we have stated, that inspired Engels above all to conceive the applicability of Hegel's ideological to materialist dialectics, stimulated significantly by the work of Darwin. As Max Adler, considered by students of socialism as one of the most authoritative writers in the field of social theory, a renowned biographer of Marx and commonly regarded as one of the principal representatives of the Austro-Marxist school, wrote: "The special merit of Engels consists in his elaboration of Marxian dialectics: that is its connection with modern natural science."[63] It is only with reference to natural science that one can fully understand Engels' recurring definition of materialist dialectics in his "Anti-Duehring." For Engels dialectics was nothing more than the science of the general natural laws of motion and development, applied to human society and thought.[64] When Engels recapitulated mathematics and the natural sciences, as he stated in his preface to the 1885 edition of the "Anti-Duehring," he became convinced that the same dialectic laws of motion were breaking through in a maze of numerous changes in nature which also governed the

15

fortuitousness of occurrences in history.[65] Engels was certain that "an exact representation of the universe, of its evolution, of the development of mankind, and of the reflection of this evolution in the minds of men, could therefore only be obtained by the methods of dialectics with its constant regard for the innumerable actions and reactions of life and death, of progressive changes."[66]

Also significant was Engels' letter to Marx on May 30, 1873, when he explained how suddenly one day he had grasped the interrelationship between dialectics and the natural sciences. As in dialectics, Engels explained, the object of natural science was moving matter or bodies. The only criterion for differentiating between bodies, besides their motion, was their relationship to other bodies. Investigation of relationships and motions was the prime purpose of natural science. Engels commented on what he called "mechanical" motion, on the laws of motion and gravitation, planetary motions in astronomy, equilibrium and contacts of moving bodies, the factors creating warmth, light, electricity, the laws of magnetism, physics, chemistry and biology—in all of these Engels hoped to discover possibilities of proving the existence of the dialectic character of natural processes,[67] a task which he recognized to be gigantic.[68] In fact, his "Anti-Duehring," with its many references to mathematics and the natural sciences, was essentially Engels' first application of dialectic materialism as a science.

In Engels' *Ludwig Feuerbach and the End of Classical German Philosophy* one finds a similar recognition of his grasp for the relationship between natural science and dialectics: Due to the great progress made by science, Engels asserted, man was able, for the first time in history, to establish intelligible and comprehensive interconnections of *all* the sciences on the basis of empirical data which they supplied themselves. The task of furnishing a "total picture" (*Gesamtbild*) had formerly been assigned to natural philosophy. Not being able to know the true scientific facts, it had tried to fill this gap in its knowledge by building on ideas and imagination. Today, however, where one needed only to arrive at a satisfactory "system of nature," today, when dialectics had won a clear victory over metaphysics,

16

philosophy of nature was abolished forever. Any attempt of reviving it was not only superfluous but a clear case of retrogression.[69]

Engels never ceased to engage in studies of the natural sciences and planned to compose a comprehensive work on dialectics in nature. For reasons of time, however, he did not get further than writing the preface and a few drafts for the first chapters. This fragmentary work was published first in 1925 in the Soviet Union and in Germany in 1927 under the title of *Dialektik der Natur* (Dietz Verlag, 1958). It was designed to prove that materialist dialectics was the only correct method in natural science.

As Engels wrote,

For . . . the (advanced) stage of natural science, when all distinctions . . . flow into the same channel, when all contrasts are mitigated by (establishing) connecting links, the old metaphysical method of thinking cannot be sustained any longer. Dialectics, which does not know any hard and fast lines, nor absolute "either-ors," which mitigates rigid metaphysical cleavages and recognizes, next to the "either-ors," also the (existence) of the "this, as well as that!" and reconciles conflicting ideas, (this dialectics) is ultimately the only proper method of thinking.[70]

In the *Dialectics of Nature* Engels examined comprehensively the history of natural sciences, particularly from the time of the Renaissance to the middle of the nineteenth century, pointing out how their development was principally determined by the modes of production. In the discussion on the reciprocal relationship and the dependence between philosophy and the natural sciences, Engels asserted that because of the progress made by the natural sciences the metaphysical conception had become wholly obsolete, as they became freed from "Hegelian mysticism." [71]

Developing his theses of dialectic materialism related to matter and motion, space and time, Engels demonstrated that the dialectic laws, as real laws of development of nature, were also applicable to the theoretical study of natural science.

A major portion of his *Dialectics of Nature* comprised the

classification of motion or processes of matter, related to the sciences which were formed to explore them. Engels distinguished between mechanical, physical, chemical and biological forms of motions, indicating for each science how it was subject to motions and processes by which they were changed and transformed dialectically from a lower to a higher form of existence.[72] As Engels stated, each science was classifiable on the basis of its peculiar, separate form of motion or on the basis of a series of related forms of motions, changes and reactions (e.g., the motion of physical bodies which, by touching one another, generated pressure, statics, hydrostatics and gases; friction and thrust produced sound, warmth, light, electricity and magnetism).[73]

Analyzing each branch of the natural sciences, Engels sought and claimed to have discovered dialectics in operation, in the form of changes of relationships: mathematics was related to apriorism of mathematical abstractions, astronomy to the development of the solar system, physics to the doctrine of transformation of energies, chemistry to the problem of the rise and essence of life, cellular theory to Darwinism, and by application of natural to the social sciences the changes and impacts of labor conditions to the development of man.

In essence, Engels' *Dialectics of Nature* was to demonstrate the role of the theoretical thinking, the material dialectics, as the key to all knowledge. It is most comprehensively stated in Engels' preface to the second edition of the *Anti-Duehring* and rendered here in full, as follows:

It goes without saying that my recapitulation of mathematics and the natural sciences was undertaken in order to convince myself also in details—of what in general I was not in doubt—that in nature, amid the welter of innumerable changes, the same dialectic laws of motion force their way through as those which in history govern the apparent fortuitousness of events; the same laws as those which similarly form the thread running through the history of the development of human thought and gradually rise to consciousness in the mind of man . . . It goes without saying that the old natural philosophy—in spite of its value and

18

the many fruitful seeds it contained—was unable to satisfy us. As is more fully brought out in this book, natural philosophy, particularly in the Hegelian form, erred because it did not concede to nature any development in time, any "succession," but only "co-existence" . . . . To me there could be no question of building the laws of dialectics into nature, but of discovering them in it and evolving them from it.[74]

For a better understanding of our appraisal of Engels it seems important to mention also his statement contained in the preface to the 1885 edition of his *Anti-Duehring,* that the understanding of the dialectic and materialist concept of nature required a thorough knowledge of mathematics and natural science. Marx, Engels wrote, was a profound mathematician, but neither one of them could keep up with the natural sciences except piecemeal and intermittently. It was *he* (Engels) who upon retiring from business (the Company of Ermen & Engels in Manchester) and moving to London (September 20, 1870) was able to find the time, in his own significant words, as far as possible for him to go through a complete "moulting" (*Mauserung*) in mathematics and the natural sciences, to which he devoted the best part of the next eight years (primarily after 1873). Since Engels claims that Marx and he were pretty much the only people who had rescued dialectics from the German idealist philosophy and had applied it to the materialist conception of nature and history, Engels actually proclaimed himself (although by implication only) to be the one expert of the two in the dialectic interpretation of the natural sciences. (Marx was pre-occupied at that time with his *Kapital*).[75]

Few philosophies have lent themselves to adaptations by political movements as readily as Hegel's. Both Marxism and Fascism found it feasible to take from his teachings such ideas as anti-liberalism, conservatism, political idealism, nationalism, and the doctrine of evolution and revolution. The possibility of interpreting Hegel in more than one direction began almost immediately after his death in 1831, when two major philosophical groups, revolutionary and conservative, claimed to be the rightful heirs of and successors to Hegel.[76]

Engels was among the claimants to Hegel's heritage, and, as a young man in the company of the "Young Hegelians," such as David Friedrich Strauss, Ludwig Feuerbach, Heinrich Heine, Edgar Bauer and others he wrote:

> The Young Germany has passed; the Young-Hegelian school has arrived. Strauss, Feuerbach, Bauer . . . have focused the general attention upon themselves. The battle of principles is at the peak of blossoming. It is a matter of life or death. Christianity is at stake; the political movement engages all.[77]

In similar references to the Young Hegelian movement Engels seemingly identified himself with it, particularly when it reached beyond theology and philosophy, i. e., beyond the original boundaries of Hegel's ideological system itself. As Max Adler in his biography of Marx and Engels put it, "What attracted both . . . was precisely a certain realistic tendency of Hegel's philosophy (challenging them) to dare the attempt to demonstrate reality as a necessity." [78]

No doubt exists that Hegel's dialectics, in particular, left a *permanent* imprint upon Engels who shared his view that all appearances had to be studied from the angle of their genesis, evolution and dissolution. By borrowing from Hegel's dialectics, Engels attempted to show the existence of laws underlying physical and human society and to prove the impact of clashes of opposing forces (interest) on their development.[79]

One of Marx's major stages in the process of transition from idealism to materialism is found in his "Aus der Kritik der Hegelschen Rechtsphilosophie," written in the summer of 1843, the introduction of which was published in the *Deutsch-Franzoesische Jahrbuecher*. The manuscript was intended to serve as a critical analysis of Hegel's *Grundlimien der Philosophie des Rechts* (Outlines of the Philosophy of Law).[80] In essence, Marx's criticism of Hegel was that not the state should be considered the center of all political existence, but the society, in which was contained all that was necessary to discern about human development. As

20

Marx stated about his study on Hegel, "My investigation resulted in the conclusion that legal as well as political forms cannot be conceived by themselves nor by the so-called general development of the human mind, but are rooted rather in the material condition of life which must be sought . . . in the anatomy of the civil society in the political economy." [81] In Marx's introduction to his "Kritik" he advised the Germans to destroy their dreamy images of non-existing conditions and to submit to criticism their abstractions on legal and political philosophy. Marx condemned the tendency of German speculative philosophy of state as being "abstract, extravagant" thinking in which reality remained a matter of the life to come.[82] As a result of the abstraction of the state, man was left dissatisfied. Summarizing his findings, Marx urged Germans to free themselves from absolutist theory and mystification and to adopt the standpoint instead that man alone was the concrete and real foundation of the state.[83]

Similarly, Engels characterized ideology when he wrote to Franz Mehring in reference to his essay "On Historical Materialism" on July 14, 1893:

Ideology is a process accomplished by the so-called thinker consciously, it is true, but with a false consciousness. The real motive forces impelling him remain unknown to him; otherwise it simply would not be an ideological process. Hence he imagines false or seeming motive forces. Because it is a process of thought he derives its form as well as its content from pure thought, either his own or that of his predecessors. He works with mere thought material, which he accepts without examination as the product of thought, and does not investigate further for a more remote source independent of thought; indeed this is a matter of course to him, because, as all action is *mediated* by thought, it appears to him to be ultimately *based* upon thought.

An answer to the questions as to why *Engels* disassociated himself later from Hegel and ultimately from his "left-wing" disciples, the Young Hegelians, may be found in Engels' own writing. It is contained in his preface to a reprint of Marx's

21

"Disclosure in the Communist Trials in Cologne" ("Enthuel-lungen ueber den Kommunistenprozess zu Koeln"). In this brief preface, written in London on October 8, 1885, Engels described how he had suddenly become aware of the extremely limited role economics had been permitted to play heretofore in the writing of history, although economics should have been recognized as a decisive factor, at least in the modern world. It had dawned upon him, Engels added, that it was economics which had formed the foundation for the rise of contemporary class conflicts. These class conflicts, particularly in England with its modern industrial development, had come to form the foundation of the political party system and therefore of its entire political history. Marx had reached this same general-ized conclusion, he asserted, as early as 1844 when he pointed out in his *Deutsch-Franzoesische Jahrbuecher* that the state did not condition bourgeois society, but that society conditioned the state, and that politics and history should be explained in terms of economic relationships. When Engels visited Marx in Paris in the summer of 1844, he found that complete agreement on all theoretical grounds "existed between them and that from that time on dates our common work."[84]

In deference to his lifetime friend, Engels credited this dis-covery which "revolutionized" the science of history essentially to Marx.[85] Engels recognized the immediate importance of their new theory for the contemporary labor movement.

No longer need he interpret the labor movement in terms of mere accident. He could now explain it as the result of the suppression of the proletarian class and also as part of the pattern in the historically necessary battle against the ruling class, the bourgeoisie. This modern class war differed from all previous ones in that the proletariat could not win its emancipation without a complete emancipation of all classes, to end all class struggles. Communism, Engels reasoned, ceased to be a fantasy of an ideal society and became instead a realistic approach to the very heart, conditions and ultimate goals of the proletarian campaign.[86] "We became compelled," Engels wrote, "to offer scientific proof for our view."[87] All previous theoretical concepts thereby came to an end. "It was more and more recognized in London that Marx *and I* were right with *our* new theory." (underscoring supplied.)[88]

Engels' assertion that the idea of historical materialism was a work of collaboration with Marx was again expressed when he wrote in 1845:

> When we met again in Brussels in the spring of 1845 Marx had already fully developed his materialist theory of history in its major features and we started to work out the details of the newly gained conception in all its ramifications.[89]

This seems to us an understatement in view of Engels' theoretical accomplishments and approximation (e.g. in his "The Position of the Workingman in England" in 1845) toward the idea of materialism before his acquaintance with Marx. Engels' position in the above quote can be explained perhaps by the fact that his recognition of the economic foundation of ideology did not become a fundamental and general theory of society until Marx had developed his analysis of the capitalist society.

Assuming that Engels' earlier contribution to the materialist conception was not commensurate with the maturity which his later collaboration with Marx produced on the subject, one must observe that Marx himself called Engels' "Outlines for a Critique of National Economy," published in Paris in the *Deutsch-Franzoesische Jahrbuecher* in February 1844 and containing substantial application of the materialist concept in criticizing the capitalist system, an "ingenious sketch in the critique of economic categories." [90]

In addition to Engels' aforementioned "sudden" grasp of the essence and significance of the materialist conception, his abandonment of ideology has been explained in terms of his strong reactions to the socio-economic changes in the industrial scene in England and the resultant effects on the working classes. These vivid facts may have made him realize the need for transforming philosophical idealism into scientific socialism.[91] This conclusion is borne out by Engels' writings in that period in which he placed himself and his readers in the center of the social movement in contemporary England.[92] Engels' description of the English proletariat stands in stark contrast to that of his "Letters from the

Wuppertal": While in the latter he put the blame mainly upon the "senseless" and mismanaging industrialists, the condition of the proletariat in Britain was blamed upon capitalism. It was not any more the case of the bourgeoisie subjectively; it became the inherent objective defect of the capitalist mode of production which had created the proletariat and its depressed social condition. Engels' strong impressions may indeed have been instrumental in helping him to realize that Hegel had failed to extend his dialectic process from the realm of pure thought to that of society, economics and politics.[93]

One of the clearest formulations of Marx and Engels delineating the contrast between idealism and materialism, particularly as applied to the interpretation of history, is found in *The German Ideology* (*Die deutsche Ideologie*), which they decided to compose in the spring of 1845 and completed it essentially by the summer of 1846. We do not possess any definite means of determining how much credit can be given to Marx and to Engels for their respective responsibility for the ideas expressed in the *German Ideology*. Engels' biographer, Gustav Mayer, admits candidly that of all other periods of their collaboration this one (between 1845 and 1846) is the most difficult for the purpose of ascertaining their separate contributions to a common enterprise in which they elaborated systematically for the first time on the theme of historical conceptions. Mayer fails to substantiate his allegation that by far the largest portion of the first part of the *German Ideology* was written by Engels and that Marx merely furnished insertions and corrections to it.[94] According to Marx's preface to his "Critique of the Political Economy," written in London in January 1859,

> Friedrich Engels had reached with me the same conclusion, . . . (on materialism) although through a different way (of reasoning), and when he also took residence in Brussels in the spring of 1845 we decided to work out together (gemeinschaftlich) the difference of our view toward the ideological German philosophy.[95]

In the *German Ideology* Marx and Engels directed their critique against the idealism of Hegel and the Young Hegelians. as well as against the "incomplete" materialism of Feuerbach who for Marx and Engels still adhered excessively to meta-physics.[96]

A few pertinent statements may suffice here to indicate how the materialist conception of history emerged in Marx's and Engels' theories. Using such strong terms as "decomposition" of the Hegelian process and a "rotting of the absolute spirit," Marx and Engels accused German philosophers of having permitted themselves to be engulfed and governed by the absolutes of religion and theology. Gradually, they had come to assume that all relationships *presupposed* the rule of religion. Ultimately they had reached the point of *explaining* all historical relationships as religious relationships. It had never occurred to them, Marx and Engels observed, to inquire into the correlation between philosophy and reality and into the correlation with their own material environment.[97] Idealistic conceptions of history had sought categories and had, therefore, never rested on the ground of reality.[98] All previous conceptions of history had almost completely neglected to probe into the real basis of the data. Instead of looking at material and worldly circumstances, these philosophers had preferred to conceive of history as a spiritual, other-worldly phenomenon. Thus misconceived, history became a sequence of religious and theoretical occurrences; history deteriorated into illusionary, erroneous fictions and unrelated gatherings of facts.[99] The Hegelian ideological historical approach, i.e., the product of theory, ideology and philosophy, in recognizing the overlordship of the mind, denied empiricism and materialism. Mysticism, speculation, dogmatic dreams and distortion were then introduced in order to create some form of order in the confusion of conflicting ideas.[100]

Engels' objections to the German (Hegelian) philosophical conception of history may best be illustrated and summarized by citing a brief passage from the *German Ideology,* in which Marx and Engels lashed out at Max Stirner, German philosopher, Young Hegelian and ideological anarchist, in the following words:

Here in Saint Max we find a splendid example (of German philosophical idealism). The speculative idea, the abstract notion becomes the moving power of history and

25

therefore history is made into mere history of philosophy. But not even this is (clearly) conceived, i.e., as occurrences based on existing sources, not to mention as effects of real historical circumstances, but is conceived and presented by the newer German philosophers, particularly Hegel and Feuerbach. And again from these presentations themselves only those are picked out which can be made to fit the immediate purpose and are suitable to our Saint. History thus becomes a mere account of alleged ideas, a witches' and ghost-story.[101]

Yet, on a number of occasions, we find Engels softening his criticism of Hegel's conception of history and writing a tone of regret. Hegel, he would argue, did not apply his dialectics consistently to the materialist history of the development of mankind, in the sense that the materialist history had conditioned the ideological, and not its reverse.[102]

What in partial restatement, was Engels' historical materialist conception of history? Most of his contributions to materialism (in co-operation with Marx) are contained in the *German Ideology,* in which the following summary is based. Essentially, historical materialism is concerned with human beings and their actual and material conditions of life, insofar as they are empirically ascertainable. According to the *German Ideology* all writing of history must commence with the natural condition of man and the modifications of that condition by human action. This necessitates a knowledge of geology, climate, means of livelihood, raw materials, and the like. The mode of life of a given group of people, Marx and Engels asserted, will coincide with their mode of production, with *what* they produce and *how* they produce. "What individuals are, depends on the material condition of their *production."* Production is also conditioned by relationships *within* populations. Relationships *among* nations are determined by the individual nations' capacities for production, division of labor, economic advances, etc.[103] All social and political relationships must be appraised empirically and without abstraction, philosophical speculation or mystification, with reference to modes of production which condition the life-process of the individual and his society.[104]

26

As it reads in the *German Ideology*, "the production of ideas, conceptions . . . is immediately interwoven with the material activity and the material relationships of men; (it is) the language of real life." [105] All thinking and acting, politics, laws, morality, religion, metaphysics, etc., of a people are directly determined by material circumstances. Men are the governors of their thinking processes, but they are, in turn, governed by the specific development of the productive forces. In direct contrast, therefore, to the Hegelian philosophy which idealized relationships, the "true process of life is placed in the center and from it the ideologies are derived as mere reflexes and echoes." [106] Morality, religion, and metaphysics had no claim to autonomous existence, reasoned Engels, but were exposed to changes brought about by material conditions. Intellectual seclusion, fantastic fixations, the empty talk of conscience and all abstractions separated from the world of reality, ceased to exist and are replaced by "real knowledge." [107] The historian who grasps historical materialism, therefore, should develop all history from the productive process, based on the material production of real life. [108]

Engels' historian therefore stands squarely on the ground of reality and must inevitably come to the conclusion that ideas and matters of the mind are the result of the overthrow of social relationships, of revolutions, which are superior to religion, philosophy and theory. [109] Applying this approach to communism, we must see that it is the existing world that must be revolutionized and modified in order to meet actual and changing needs. [110]

We can find further clarification of Engels' views in a letter he wrote in reply to Heinz Starkenburg, a German social-democrat. Starkenburg had inquired about the extent to which economic conditions were the casual factors in comparison with the part played by *racial* elements and by historical personalities:

What we understand by the economic conditions which we regard as the determining basis of the history of society are the methods by which human beings in a given society produce their means of subsistence and exchange the products among themselves . . . This technique also determines the method of exchange and, further, the division of products, and with it, after the dissolution of tribal society, the division into classes also and hence the relations of lordship and servitude and with them the state, politics, law, etc. Under economic conditions are further included the geographical basis on which they operate . . . If technique depends largely on the state of science, science depends far more still on the *state* and the requirements of technique. If society has a technical need, that helps science forward more than ten universities . . . We regard economic conditions as the factor which ultimately determines historical development. But race is itself an economic factor . . . Political, juridical, philosophical, religious, literary, artistic, etc., development is based on economic development. But all these react upon one another and also upon the economic base. It is not that the economic position is the *cause and alone active,* while everything else has only a passive effect. There is rather, interaction on the basis of the economic necessity, which *ultimately* always asserts itself . . . Men make their history themselves, but not as yet with a collective will or according to a collective plan or even in a definitely defined, given society. Their efforts clash, and for that very reason all such societies are governed by *necessity,* which is supplemented by and appears under the forms of *accident.* The necessity which here asserts itself amidst all accident is again ultimately economic necessity. This is where the so-called great men come in for treatment. That such and such a man and precisely that man arises at that particular time in that given country is of course pure incident. But cut him out and there will be a demand for a substitute . . . in the long run he will be found.[111]

Perhaps Engels' best definition of the materialist concept of history is contained in "The Development of Socialism" and reads as follows:

The materialist conception of history proceeds from the proposition that production and the exchange of products, after production, is the basis of all social order; that in every historically appearing society the distribution of products and with it the social organization into classes or estates is determined by what is produced and how that which is produced is exchanged. Therefore, the ultimate causes of all societal changes and political revolutions are to be sought not in the minds of men, not in their growing insights into eternal truth and justice, but in the changes of the modes of production and exchange; they are to be sought not in philosophy, but in the economy of the respective epoch.[112]

Evidence exists that Engels was willing to make exceptions to the rule of primacy of the economic materialist conception by admitting that the economic factor was not the only active and automatic one in the cause of historical processes. Thus he stated in a letter from London in September 21-28, 1890, to Joseph Bloch, editor-in-chief of a socialist journal:

According to the materialist conception of history, the *ultimately* determining element in history is the production and reproduction of real life. More than this neither Marx nor I have ever asserted. Hence if somebody twists this into saying that the economic element is the *only* determining one, he transforms that proposition into a meaningless, abstract, senseless phrase. The economic situation is the basis, but the various elements of the superstructure—political forms of the class struggle and its results, to wit: constitutions established by the victorious class after a successful battle, etc., juridical forms, and even the reflexes of all these actual struggles in the brains of the participants, political, juristic, philosophical theories, religious views, and their further development into systems of dogmas—also exercise their influence upon the course of the historical struggles and in many cases preponderate in determining their *form*. There is an interaction of all these elements in which, amidst all the endless hosts of accidents . . . the economic movement finally asserts itself as necessary . . .[113]

Engels explained in the same letter that, although economic circumstances were ultimately decisive being "the strongest, and most primordial," political ones and even tradition had a place. There were "innumerable intersecting forces, infinite series of parallelograms of forces which co-determined all historical events."[114]

29

Engels fully realized that an analysis of the development of the materialist conception would require many years of intense study. He was aware that only massive, critically-oriented, completely mastered historical material could lead to the solution of such a task.[115] "All history must be studied afresh," wrote Engels to Conrad Schmidt from London, August 5, 1890. "The conditions of existence of the different formations of society must be individually examined before the attempt is made to deduce from them the political, civil-legal, aesthetic, philosophical, religious, etc., notions corresponding to them . . . In this field we can utilize masses of help . . . "[116]

Engels acknowledged that there were definite limits to the study of the materialist conception of history. In his introduction to "The Class Wars in France, 1848 to 1850 of Karl Marx," (edition 1895), he admitted that one could never go back to the last economic cause. A clear grasp of the economic history of a given period could only be obtained subsequently, never contemporaneously, and only after the complete collection and sifting of the required material.[117] The materialist method could only reach to the presently existing circumstances of classes and societies, and thus was forced to base its judgment of past economics on the circumstances of the present time. This system was inevitably subject to some error and miscalculation, Engels asserted.[118]

In many of his writings, Engels applied his materialist approach to concrete situations, contrasting his approach with that of the idealist, Hegelian school. For instance, in discussing the history of German national unification, Engels pointed out its essentially material foundations. It was not, he wrote, a matter of German courage and soul-struggle; not a mystified, sentimental students' movement; not a romantic medieval revivalism; not the appeal by liberal ideologists to adopt Swiss cantonal republicanism to Germany: but a clear case of economic necessities motivating businessmen and industrialists to demand free commerce and trade, and the removal of the obsolete small-state system that was typical of Germany before the unification.[119]

It is beyond the scope of this study to list all the evidence in Engels' writings for his application of the materialist method.

It is clearly recognizable in Engels' descriptions, analyses of causes, courses of actions and results of the "German Peasants' War," and in his "Revolution and Counterrevolution in Germany (1851-52)" which dealt with the revolutionary wars of 1848 and 1849. It is also evident in his analysis of social and political conditions of England in his essay on the "Position in England," which discussed class problems, parties, parliamentarianism, constitutionalism, industrial production and property relationships. Further examples of Engels' application of the materialist method are to be found in his many studies of military science (including revolutions, wars, and the theory and art of war); in his discussion on housing conditions and the contrast between urban and rural conditions of his times; and in his numerous references to the relationship between law and economics.[120]

It was Engels' contention that historical materialism was not a monopoly of the modern socialist movement. In fact he cited a number of historical events where "bourgeois" writers had taken recourse to historical materialism. Thus he asserted in his introduction to the English edition of "Socialism: Utopian and Scientific," published in 1892, that England from the seventeenth century onwards was "the original home of all modern materialism. Materialism is the natural-born son of Great Britain."[121] According to Engels, Francis Bacon was "the real progenitor of English materialism," because he considered natural philosophy to be the only true philosophy and because he referred back to Greek natural scientists such as Anaxagoras and Democritus for his authorities. Hobbes and Locke, too, were listed by Engels as being advocates of materialism, along with those in the nineteenth century who approved of materialism via religious agnosticism. Thus, Engels concluded, British respectability would not honestly feel shocked when he used the term "historical materialism" to designate that view of the course of history which seeks the ultimate cause and great moving power of all important historical events in the economic development of society, in the changes in the modes of production and exchange, in the consequent division of society into classes, and in the struggle of these classes against one another.[122]

31

CHAPTER III

PEACEFUL SOLUTIONS VERSUS
REVOLUTIONARY TRANSFORMATION

Engels' sojourn in England in the 1840's coincided with the rise of the Chartist movement. Engels studied the movement and attended Chartist conferences and meetings, associating himself with their cause. He was sympathetic towards Chartism, but critical of certain aspects of their program. Above all he criticized their method of working peacefully toward socialist ends ("legal revolution"). Repeatedly in his writings, he pointed out that, since proletarian movements had been suppressed in most states, the proletariat would be forced into revolution. The pressure between the classes, becoming unbearable, would result in violent explosion, as the position of the swelling ranks of the proletarians would encounter an enormous increase of bourgeois wealth and productivity.[123] Commenting on an unsuccessful Chartist revolution in Manchester in the summer of 1842, Engels concluded that social evils could not be cured by "people's charters."[124] Understandably, it was only with the Chartist radical wing that Engels could identify himself.[125] For him, the concept of revolution by peaceful means was an impossibility; only a violent transformation of the existing conditions could improve the position of the proletarians. It would have to be a political, as well as a social revolution.[126]

Engels rejected equally the doctrine of gradualism in England as advocated by the Fabian socialists, founded in 1884 largely by middle-class intellectuals of the caliber of Sidney Webb. In a letter to Karl Kautsky on September 4, 1892, in which he condemned the Fabian affiliation of the workers with the liberals, he referred to the Fabians as a "clique of bourgeois 'socialists' of diverse caliber, from careerists to sentimental socialists and philanthropists." He accused Fabians of employing corrupt parliamentary means, i.e., money, intrigue and careerism. He also criticized them for restricting their leadership to the educated classes, with only a token inclusion of workers in the ranks of the Fabians.[127]

Similarly Engels upbraided the Fabians in his letter to Friedrich Sorge, a German labor leader and friend of Marx and Engels, on January 18, 1893. Engels ridiculed the "ambitious" Fabians who were kind enough to set themselves at the head of a social revolution, even though "fear of revolution" was their fundamental principle. Fabian socialists, Engels asserted, were an extreme but inevitable consequence of bourgeois liberalism. They had set themselves the task not of opposing, but of permeating liberalism with socialism. In that pursuit, Engels stated, Fabians either lied, deceived themselves, or else betrayed socialism. At the critical moment many of their followers would "certainly fall away." [128]

On the continent, singled out in Engels' attack on those who sought peaceful solutions for socialism were the "reactionary" German Social-Democrats. As Engels wrote, they were "typical" German theorists and sentimental petty-bourgeois.[129] They looked at social democracy as an end in itself rather than merely a state of transition to communism; and they felt it was sufficient for solving the ills of the existing situation of the proletariat. They were either proletarians, who could be accused of ignorance, or they were petty-bourgeois, who could not on any account be identified with the proletarians. In either case, they were "reactionary." [130]

As we have pointed out above, Engels could not conceive of harmony of interests existing between capitalism and labor. It was on this ground that Engels also rejected philanthropy on the part of the capitalist, as for instance in the form of providing inexpensive housing for the workers (the "cottage system"). He expected only bribery and deception from philanthropy, which he considered to be forms of fraud and speculation under the guise of humanitarianism and altruism. Whatever the motive, philanthropy generally had amounted to so little that the British Parliament, when it reported on the position of the laborers, did not see fit to include philanthropic projects in its parliamentary reports.[131]

A form of philanthropy which Engels was more willing to accept was that which the English Utopian socialists espoused. Engels had established contact with them and became a contributor to their periodical, *The New Moral World*. He frequently commented in his articles on the Continental European Utopian socialists. Several passages in Engels' writings revealed a definite appreciation for their thoughts and actions. Thus he praised Henry de Saint-Simon for being among the first to recognize that only a small fraction of the Third Estate, the bourgeoisie, had benefited from the victory of the French Revolution, and for having made the distinction between the "idle" and the "workers." In the end the "idle" would lose spiritual and political leadership according to Saint-Simon. Engels also gave him credit for his "ingenious" discovery of a class struggle underlying the French Revolution, and for anticipating the recognition of the economic basis of all political institutions.[132]

Charles Fourier's Utopianism was also commended by Engels for its deeply penetrating critique of existing social conditions, and for pointing out the discrepancy between the misery of the actually existing bourgeois world and the glowing promises of the former rationalists and contemporary bourgeois ideologists.[133] Equally praised were Robert Owen's contributions to socialism considered by Engels as being among the "most practical and most elaborated" proposals, such as the plan for a community housing project.[134] In addition, the Utopian emphasis on the psychological effect of the capitalist system and the proposed psychological solutions for workers were mentioned favorably by Engels.[135]

However, this was as far as Engels would go in giving recognition to Utopianism. His objections outweighed his approvals. Repeatedly Engels pointed out the differences of approach which separated the scientific from the Utopian socialists. For instance, while Pierre-Joseph Proudhon's utopianism planned for transfer of property to the individual workers, Engels advocated that all property remain the collective property of the working class.[136] While Utopians claimed to liberate all mankind without appealing to any particular class, Engels purposely appealed only to the class-conscious proletariat.[137] While Owen's utopianism intended to smooth over the contrast between bourgeoisie and proletariat, recommended tame and peaceful methods, stressed philanthropy and universal love, and underscored socialism with erudite and metaphysical arguments, Engels stood for almost the exact opposite; above all, he insisted that socialism should remain a genuine proletarian working class movement, cleansed from all bourgeois elements.[138]

Utopianism was based too much on notions of absolute truth, reason and justice, as Engels pointed out in his *"Development,"* and would therefore by the nature of these abstractions always be interpreted differently and subjectively during different eras and by different individuals. The unavoidable consequence would be, wrote Engels, a sort of "eclectic average-socialism," with many different shades and mixtures of arguments, economic doctrines and social plans for the future in the minds of various sectarian utopian founders. "In order to make socialism a science, it had to be put first on the realistic (non-utopian) basis." [139]

Engels' objections to utopianism frequently concentrated on the errors of rationalism applied to society and government, expounded primarily by the French *philosophes* in the eighteenth century.[140] Rousseau's and others' ideas on the social contract and on solutions to social problems from whose ideas utopianism derived many of its own ideas may have succeeded, according to Engels, in breaking the fetters of feudalism, but only transferred the rights and privileges of the feudal society to the bourgeoisie, the working masses falling by the wayside, and the smaller merchants and peasants gaining "freedom *from* property," rather than "freedom of property," as they had hoped for.[141] The newly arising social problems which bourgeois rationalism created for the economy of Europe were instrumental, Engels alleged, in calling in existence the various utopian excogitations with their belief in the perfectibility and sociability of man, recommending changes of the social order by societal experiments. For Engels these were "stupendously grand thoughts," "germs of thought." [142] He refused to talk down on the utopian fantasies and was prepared to condone them because of the fact that they could not be anything else at the time, the capitalist mode of production still being largely undeveloped. "They necessarily had to construct the elements of a new society out of their own heads, because within the old society the elements of the new were not as yet generally apparent." [143]

As we have seen, Engels' studies in the natural sciences and his adoption and adaptation of Hegel's dialectics provided the two factors upon which he based his contributions to "scientific socialism." These two factors were outlined in his "Anti-Duehring," in which the laws of the communist revolutionary transformation of the world were set forth.

In addition, writing to Marx from Manchester, England, on July 14, 1858, Engels described, perhaps most clearly, his concept of the psychological and physical transitions and transformations in the following passage:

> The cell is Hegel's 'being-in-itself' and its development exactly follows the Hegelian process, resulting finally in the 'idea,' i.e., each completed organism. Another result which would have pleased old Hegel is the correlation of forces in physics: the law that under given conditions mechanical motion . . . is changed into heat, heat into light, light into chemical affinity, chemical affinity . . . into electricity, electricity into magnetism . . .[144]

Engels' rule of transition and transformation was extended also to political society by drawing parallels between dialectics in natural science, philosophy and politics. Socialism ceased to be the accidental discovery of outstanding thinkers and became instead "the necessary product of a battle between historically formed classes, the proletariat and the bourgeoisie." [145] "The new facts compelled us to re-examine all past history, and thereupon it was shown that all previous history, with the exception of primeval times, was a history of class struggle." [146]

What the cell was for physiology, what the correlation of forces was for physics, what the "Hegelian process" was for philosophy—the idea of dialectically conditioned conflict of classes was for political society,—conflict which would end only with the ending of all class differences themselves. And nothing could deter Engels' belief in the inevitability of the coming of the classless communist society, even when it was objected that communism was unrealizable because man could never cooperate with his fellow-man communistically, that man by nature would always want easy rather than difficult work, would strive for higher property and status rather than consent to egalitarianism. In his article on the "Description of the newly established and still existing Communist Settlements," by referring to successful experiments in religious sectarian settlements, Engels defended communism as having worked in practice, in settlements, in fact, which could not even be classified as politically communist.[147] If communist experiments had worked out on a smaller scale in communist and sectarian model communities, they would work out on national scale, too, Engels assumed, because the principle of communist community life had proved to be sound.

The work of building a communist society must be the collective work of the workers, not of the bourgeoisie or of bourgeois-sponsored philanthropy. The only way, reasoned Engels, that the workers could improve their position and end their exploitation was by eliminating the bourgeoisie, which would always defend its own interests with all means. Only by guided hatred and rebellion against the bourgeoisie could the workers save themselves.[148] Any form of cooperation with the bourgeoisie within the framework of the state was an illusion doomed to failure.[149] When the bourgeoisie ceased to be progressive and revolutionary itself, as it had after the French Revolution, the working class must take over the leadership from it.[150]

There could be no identification between workers and capitalists. Separation of labor and private property made such identification an impossibility, and with this separation the interest of the individual or the family was bound to be at variance with the common interest of all.[151] As long as labor was considered inferior to capital, property would rule over the former. In a communist society, however, where no social activities would be fixed and where each person could decide for himself which branch of activity he wanted to select, the conflict between interests would come to an end. The bourgeois state, the *German Ideology* reads, because it separated individual and common interests, made any real community of interests illusory.[152] History had shown that every class which had established itself had made an attempt to appear to represent the interests of all classes. Any form of apparent cooperation of classes was nothing more than involuntary. Classes would remain alien to each other as long as class differences continued to exist.[153] The only truly workable community of interests always existed within a class itself.[154] "The teachings of bourgeois economists," Engels wrote in his "Development," "of the identity of capital and labor, of the general harmony and general popular well-being as a result of free competition, have increasingly been proven by the facts to be lies." [155]

Nor did any identification exist between the workers and the members of the lower middle class. Engels rejected petty-bourgeois socialism, which claimed equality of status with proletarian socialism.[156] At most, he was ready to acknowledge that both the bourgeoisie and the proletariat were the products of a new epoch and had once both opposed the Old Regime. Yet, with their common opponent removed, the two classes faced each other antagonistically and their former solidarity of interest was forgotten. It was a tragedy for the bourgeois that by conferring civil rights on all men, by lifting restrictions on trade and commerce, and by raising the privileges and prerogatives of the upper classes, it thereby delivered weapons into the hands of the proletariat. Freedom of speech, press, and assembly, the right to vote and to join associations were eagerly taken up by the proletariat but turned against those who had granted them these rights.[157] The bourgeoisie had made enormous progress, Engels admitted when he evaluated the Revolution of 1848; but it was ultimately only blazing a trail for the proletariat. "We need you now . . . you must put the remnants of the Middle Ages and the absolute monarchy out of the way for us!" [158]

A similar idea of using the bourgeoisie as a spearhead or as the lesser of the evil, was expressed by Engels in an article he wrote as Paris correspondent for the English Chartist newspaper *Northern Star* (XI, January 22, 1848, No. 535, p. 7): "After all, the modern bourgeois, with civilization, industry, order and, at least, relative enlightenment following him, is preferable to the feudal lord or to the marauding robber, with the barbarian state of society to which they belong."[159] Once the bourgeoisie had ceased to be "useful" to the proletariat, and once the class conflict had crystallized into a confrontation of possessors and dispossessed, the battle between the bourgeoisie and the proletariat was unavoidable. The bourgeoisie and the idea of private property with it would sink down, as had previously the aristocracy and the idea of absolute monarchy.[160] History tended to repeat itself; once, Engels asserted, it had been the bourgeoisie which had fought against its socio-economic opponents, finding high-sounding justifications for itself as a battle of city versus country, industry versus landed property, and monetary economy versus natural economy.[161]

In every period of history, argued Engels, it had been the ruling class, not a community of classes, which had constituted the intellectual power. Material domination had also determined intellectual domination. Every ruling class had made its ideas the dominating ideas of its era.[162] Producers of material goods had also been producers of thoughts, that is, each ruling class had developed its own "active ideologist," who set themselves the task of creating and of perpetuating the superiority of their own class.[163] As long as separate classes continue to exist, revolutionary wars will be directed against the ruling class. Only with the advent of communism and its liquidation of all classes and nationalities will class struggle come to an end.[164]

Nor could socialism claim a monopoly on its concept of class. Engels emphasized in "The Development" that in the French Revolution a middle-class movement subjected all things, including religion, science, society and government to merciless criticism; previous standards were rejected for not fitting into the new scheme of rationality.[165] For Engels the French Revolution and its deification of rationalism was nothing more than the "idealized realm" of the bourgeoisie.[166] Equality, property, the rational state, Rousseau's social contract, democracy—all were idealized aspects of a bourgeois class ideology in disguise and with the pretext of liberating all mankind.[167] The French Revolution was the exclusive victory of the Third Estate, that is of its small privileged rank, the property-owning bourgeoisie.[168]

In his *Anti-Duehring* (Chapter X: Morality and Law. Equality), Engels expounded his theory that bourgeois egalitarianism, historically the conceptual basis of democracy, was in error because it falsely assumed that the truth in morality, laws and human equality could be obtained (like mathematics) with mathematical certainty.[169] Instead of deducing concepts from reality, bourgeois egalitarians deduced reality from ideology. This misconception, according to Engels, like all similar forms and applications of ideological construction because they were torn from real social relations, established morals and laws in the form of immutable axioms.[170] For instance, an eighteenth century principle laid down that all men were absolutely equal to one another and were as human beings neither superior nor inferior in their interrelationships.[171] For Engels this axiom totally disregarded the existing inequalities of national, economic, political, religious, sexual and personal realities. Even if a situation could be constructed (e.g., two shipwrecked people alone on an island) which gave men the opportunity of establishing among themselves a form of entire equality, eliminating injustice, tyranny or servitude, sooner or later such an equality would be upset; a Robinson Crusoe was bound to impose himself on a Friday. Cases were also cited by Engels of voluntary surrender of equality and "permissible dependence," as for instance in the relationship between children and parents, and other forms of "inadequate self-determination." [172]

More evident yet was the case of moral inequality: Engels contended that not two persons were morally entirely equal to each other. Mankind was divided sharply, he wrote, into human men and beast men, into those who acted in accordance with truth and science, and those in accordance with superstition, prejudice and perversity. Christianity itself distinguished between good and evil and separated the universe correspondingly, Engels pointed out. "The entire quality of . . . wills, exists only so long as these . . . wills will *nothing*; . . . as soon as they cease to be human wills as such, and are transformed into real, individual wills, into the wills of . . . real people, equality comes to an end." [173]

Where democratic egalitarianism made its greatest miscalculation, Engels emphasized, was when it failed to apply equality of man to equal political and social status for all men. No doubt, this was a conception for which thousands of years would have to pass (and had passed already) from the original conception of "relative" equality to the acceptance of political and social equality as something natural and self-evident.[174] Bourgeois egalitarianism was not prepared to extend its standard of equality to the realm of politics and society. Yet, the bourgeoisie could not help to create the proletariat which, at the same time that the bourgeoisie itself demanded the absolute abolition of class privileges which affected it adversely, the proletariat demanded the abolition of all class privileges, in fact, the abolition of the *classes themselves*.[175] What Engels stressed particularly in his discussion on the historical expansion of the concept of equality (from bourgeois to a people's social-democratic equality) was that

The idea of equality both in its bourgeois and in its proletarian form, is therefore itself a historical product, the creation of which required definite historical conditions that in turn themselves presuppose a long previous history. It is therefore anything but an eternal truth.[176]

Engels distrusted democracy, the last bastion of the bourgeoisie. This was bluntly expressed in his letter on March 24, 1884 to Eduard Bernstein, the known German socialist and founder of the "Revisionist" school of socialism (underscoring is Engels') :

This conception (of democracy) changes with every *demos* and so does not get us a step further. In my opinion what should be said is this: the proletariat, too, requires democratic *forms* for the seizure of political power, but, like all political forms, these serve it as means. But if we want to make democracy an *aim* to-day, then we must support ourselves upon the peasants and petty bourgeoisie, that is upon classes in process of dissolution, which, as soon as they try to maintain themselves artificially, are *reactionary* in relation to the proletariat. Furthermore it must not be forgotten that the logical form of bourgeois domination is precisely the

41

democratic republic.[177]

Democracy, for Engels, was a contradiction in itself, untruthful and hypocritical. Its promised political liberty was only pretence, in fact, the worst kind of slavery. Genuine liberty and genuine equality could come only from communism.[178] England's democracy was run by a lazy, mammonist, corrupt, worthless and soulless landed aristocracy, as Thomas Carlyle had already stated. [179] Not even in the Lower House was there a true democracy: the large majority of the working class was excluded by being disenfranchised. Political representation was a farce. Property alone ruled in England. The nature of the Constitution, Crown, Parliament, the Established Church, the court system and the law itself indicated to Engels that England in practice was void of democracy. [180]

It is needless to add that Engels objected to constitutional monarchy as well as to democratic republicanism. He held that the bourgeoisie tended to prefer constitutional monarchy to a republic as the more effective shield to the proletariat. This was formulated in his correspondence with Bernstein as follows:

The liberal constitutional monarchy is the proper form for the bourgeois rule, first, in the beginning, when the bourgeoisie has not quite finished the absolute monarchy and second, at the end, when the proletariat has begun to make the democratic republic too dangerous.[181]

Engels did not reject constitutional monarchy merely because it was the acceptable form of government to the bouregoisie, but because it was based on fear, fear of pure monarchy, fear of pure democracy, fear of man of himself.[182] He pointed out the powerlessness of the sovereign King of England, the emptiness of the powers of the Crown, as an institution, the artificiality of the monarchy in general, the hollow formality, lack of responsibility and anachronism of its supporting aristocracy.[183]

CHAPTER IV

REFORMISM VERSUS SOCIAL REVOLUTION

In a letter to August Bebel on September 17/18, 1879, Engels rejected strict adherence to peaceful and bloodless methods in attaining the socialist goal. This is one of many similar references in which he spoke against the reformists among the socialists.[184] Let the bourgeoisie fear the "Red Spectre," Engels wrote to Bebel; why not admit that war between classes is unavoidable?[185] To surrender the idea of the class struggle and to walk hand in hand with the so-called "friends of labor" would inevitably end up with the proletariat being taken-in by the bourgeoisie. Nor would it make sense to stop short of complete revolutionary overthrow or to postpone the program. After more than forty years of teaching the necessity of class war, it would be self-defeating for the proletariat to abandon it now in order to attract the support of the bourgeoisie. In any case the working class was better off without such support for its liberation.[186] If, however, members of the bourgeoisie wanted to join the revolutionary cause of the proletariat, the condition must be their complete identification with the proletariat.[187]

The fact was that "the battle is already here," Engels wrote in "The Position in England." "The Constitution is shaken in its foundations."[188] It was a battle of the poor against the rich, a battle for democracy—that is, for social democracy. This democracy, in turn, was merely a prelude to the coming socialism. Socialism meant democracy turned proletarian, one which had become a principle of the masses.[189]

Were private property to remain untouched or only partly redistributed, Engels declared in a speech at Elberfeld, this would mean failure to deal thoroughly with the basic factors causing the revolution. Sooner or later, similar conditions and the need for another revolution would re-occur. Only a total, thoroughgoing social revolution, a proclamation of communism, would do. If bloodshed were to be avoided, communism had to be instituted. One could not avoid a bloody solution without applying at least some form of the communist solution to the problems of labor. (With this Engels seemed to admit the *possibility* of a bloodless communist revolution, an admission which stood in contrast to most of his other related statements.)[190]

To examine the agreement on the principle of the inevitability and necessity of the coming revolution between Marx and Engels, the following related excerpts taken from Marx's "Zur Kritik der Hegelschen Rechtsphilosophie" will be quoted:

It is not the *radical* revolution, *universal human* emancipation, which is a utopian dream of Germany, but rather the partial, merely political, revolution, which leaves the pillars of the building intact. What is the basis of a partial, merely political revolution? Simply this: *a part of civic society* emancipates itself and attains *general* domination, a particular class, from its *particular situation,* undertakes the general emancipation of society[191].... But in Germany every class lacks not only the consistency, the incisiveness, the courage, the ruthlessness required to turn it into the negative representative of society, but also that generosity needed to identify itself, if only for a moment, with the popular mind . . . The middle class hardly dares to conceive the idea of emancipation from its own standpoint, and already the development of social conditions, and the progress of political theory, declares this standpoint to be antiquated or at least problematical.[192]

In France, partial emancipation is the basis of complete emancipation. In Germany, universal emancipation is the *conditio sine qua non* of any partial emancipation. In France it is the reality, in Germany the impossibility, of a step-by-step emancipation which must give birth to complete liberty . . . Where then is there the *positive* possibility of German emancipation? In the formation of a class with *radical chains*

44

... a class which is the dissolution of all classes, a sphere of society which has a universal character because its sufferings are universal, and which claims no *particular right* because the wrong committed against it is not a *particular wrong* but wrong *as such* . . .[193] When the proletariat declares the *dissolution of the existing order* it does no more than proclaim the *secret of its own existence,* for it constitutes the *effective* dissolution of this order . . . As philosophy finds its *material* weapons in the proletariat, so the proletariat discovers its *intellectual* weapons in philosophy, and once the lightning-flash of the idea has penetrated this naive popular soil, the emancipation of the *Germans* to *manhood* will become reality . . . The emancipation of the *German* is the emancipation of *man. Philosophy is* the *head* of this emancipation, and the *proletariat* its *heart.* Philosophy cannot realize itself without abolishing the proletariat, and the proletariat cannot emancipate itself without realizing philosophy.[194]

Concerning the coming of the social revolution an article by Engels in the *Rheinische Zeitung* pointed out the weakness and artificiality of the social and political structure of England. He had noticed a naive or ignorant attitude on the part of the English ruling classes, which, in his opinion, failed to realize the growing power of proletarian resistance. In a similar article Engels listed a number of facts and circumstances which cumulatively would result in a violent clash of classes, among them the unpopular policy of Parliament, the slighting of public opinion, the unilateral class-control of justice and administration,[196] and the failure of capitalism to solve the problem of low-income housing.[197]

Neither social, nor the political, revolution could be avoided in England.[198] The upper class of England, with its inherited political and religious prejudices, was intellectually and socially enervated. Only the worker, the pariahs of England, still possessed a future. They alone had escaped the decline of respectability, the dullness and decomposition of the "better sort of people.[199] The social revolution had been in progress in England for more than seventy or ninety years, wrote Engels on August 31, 1844, and was advancing rapidly toward its final crisis.[200]

An abundance of evidence existed to convince Engels that "the final crisis," was in the making. He had been a firsthand observer of the grim social conditions existing in England at his time, conditions which he described most realistically in "The Position of the Working Class in England." As he stated in its preface, proletarian conditions and the misery at the core of all social conditions were most "classically" developed in England. The social conditions were perhaps the same in Germany, though not equally "classical." [201] What made England the best object for social analysis was, of course, its advanced technology, a development which Engels traced to its historical roots. He began with the pre-factory stage when British workers still held a comparatively comfortable social position, and showed their almost immediate deterioration setting in shortly after James Hargreaves' invention of the spinning-jenny, Richard Arkwright's spinning-throstle and Samuel Crompton's cotton-mule. Engels described the replacement of the workers by machines, the growth of the English cotton, wool, linen and silk industries and the many additional new inventions or refinements in the various branches of industry, the impact of the steam engine, the rise of iron production, the repercussion of industrial development on agriculture and communication, the growth of cities, the power of the upper bourgeoisie, and the simultaneous decline of the lower middle class and proletariat.[202] Engels paid special attention to the social and psychological consequences of the industrial revolution upon the inhabitants of the big cities; the near-starvation wages, destitution, famine, and the generally poor conditions of food and shelter for the working class.[203]

For Engels the clearest indication of the existing social war was the effect of competition on the proletariat and capitalists alike.[204] Competition operated not only as a war between the classes, but also within each class.[205] The competition among the proletarians themselves was the most disastrous of all, because it resulted in wages being reduced to a bare minimum, as the workers became legally and actually the slaves of the propertied classes.

As Engels described it, this was one of the great paradoxes of

46

the capitalist economy: it could expand greatly producing goods at greatly lowered prices, yet at the same time, it could not expand its consumer markets sufficiently, even with lower prices, since the bulk of the consumers were the poorly paid workers themselves.[206] This cycle resulted in the recurrence of economic crisis, unemployment and further destitution of the unemployed.[207]

Engels drew significant conclusions from all material so far as society was concerned. In fact, a major portion of "The Position" was devoted to just this: the impact of these conditions, physically, intellectually, and morally, on the British working class.[208] Engels accused the capitalist society of "social murder" of the proletarians, their premature low-age mortality, the prevalence of contagious and epidemic diseases, malnutrition, drunkenness, general poor health, inferior and neglected education, immorality and general demoralization. Engels wrote that the workers were rejected, not only because of their low economic status, but also because of their physical, intellectual and moral inferiority, to which, however, they had been reduced by the bourgeoisie. No wonder also that the proletariat had lost all its religious faith and had turned to atheism.[209] As a final result—and Engels offered these predictive comments and descriptions—the social revolution was bound to break out, oppressed and congested as the workers were in the industrial cities. Already they were beginning

to become class-conscious in their entirety; they were becoming aware that in unison they represented a power, however weak they might be separately . . . Consciousness of their being oppressed and of their gaining social and economic importance . . . It is in the large cities that the labor movement first started, where labor first began to reflect on its condition, where the contrast between proletariat and bourgeoisie first came into appearance, and from whence labor associations, chartism and socialism proceeded . . .[210]

If the bourgeoisie failed or refused to grasp the true socio-economic situation, namely, the brewing of a violent storm, if the propertied class was so stupid and blinded by its momentary advantage, Engels concluded, "All hope for a peaceful solution of the social problem must probably be abandoned. The only possible recourse remains a violent revolution." [211]

It is safe to conclude that Engels' historical analysis of England with its socio-economic implications was also meant to apply, although to a lesser degree, to other similarly industrialized states of contemporary Europe. In fact, long before Engels ever thought of going to England and of describing English conditions, he had made a significant contribution to a socio-economic analysis of his native, industrially developed Wuppertal,[212] located in the Prussian Rhine province, as we have mentioned in another part of this study. As a recent biographer of Engels' work, E. A. Stepanowa, has observed the knowledge of poverty and misery which Engels gained in Wuppertal as a youth made a permanent impression upon him and figured in the development of his later social and political philosophy.[213]

One must understand that in the 1830's, in western Europe generally and not only in the Rhine Province, a number of major social crises had taken place, such as the July Revolution of 1830. Nevertheless, Engels could have found no other place more suited to his advanced studies in social politics than England, to which Engels went in November 1842. It was more than incidental that his first article in England began with the posing of the question: "Is a revolution possible or even probable in England?"[214] As the dedication to his book on "The Position" stated characteristically:

I want to see you in your dwellings, watch you in your daily life, talk to you about your conditions of life and sufferings, be a witness to your battles against the social and political power of your oppressors.[215]

On the matter of dimension of the coming social revolution, Engels was obscure, except for a letter to Bernstein of August 27, 1883, in which he scolded the Germans for assuming the revolution would be a matter of "overnight." It would be "a process of development," over a period of years, as every revolution had been. A hastily conducted revolution, he wrote to him, would suffice only in the case of a regime which was about to collapse by itself; in any other case, it would lead to the opposite result of what was intended by the revolution.[216] The social revolution would have to be "sweeping" ("durchgreifend"), Engels explained in an article for the *New Moral World,* affecting the fundamental structure of the social condition. The degree of thoroughness of the social revolution would depend on the *origin* of communism in each country. Engels recognized the existence of differences of opinion on *how sweeping* the revolution ought to be.[217] In any case the revolution must be carefully prepared, Engels admonished in the letter to Bernstein on August 27, 1883.[218]

It should be noted here that Engels did not conceive of revolutions or other forms of coercion as end in themselves. This position was most clearly presented in his polemics against Duehring's force theory according to which all past history could be traced to force, "historically the fundamental thing." Conversely, Engels proposed that force was only the means, while the end was economic advantage.[219] Whereas Duehring argued that property was founded on force, resulted from the forceful domination by man at the exclusion of others from the natural means of subsistence, subjugated and enslaved men, Engels asserted that subjugation of man first of all presupposed the existence of property of the instruments of labor, after which man was placed in bondage by man. In order to be in possession of property "in excess of the average," an act of force (for instance by robbery or fraud) could be assumed to precede; however, mostly property was acquired by non-coercive methods, such as by labor or trade. The study of early primitive communes revealed to Engels that property, which existed as part of any civilized order, resulted from an exchange of commodities, produced for the purpose of exchange. There was no act of force but "voluntariness and custom" involved in the process, nor was it when the community lands were divided up and changed into private ownership.[220] When in a much later stage of economic development property became concentrated in the hands of a small class and the majority degraded into propertyless proletarians, even then force played an insignificant part in it at all, but resulted, according to Engels, from purely economic causes.[221] When capitalism came into existence and created a new class, the proletariat, it was impelled as a purely economic result to drive its own system, its new "economic situation," toward ruin. It was the economic situation which for Engels was the decisive cause of the political situation, not that conversely the political situation could be artificially changed (e.g., by force) in order to create a new economic situation:[222]

The role played in history by force as contrasted with economic development is therefore clear. In the first place, all political power is originally based on an economic, social, function, and increases in proportion as the members of society, through the dissolution of the primitive community, become transformed into private producers and thus become more and more divorced from the administrators of the common functions of society.[223]

Would the state remain after the revolution had occurred? "The Development" contains the answer to this question, which we prefer to quote in full because of its significance:

Proletarian Revolution, dissolution of contradictions: The proletariat seizes the public power and, through it, transforms the social means of production, which are slipping out of the hands of the bourgeoisie into public property. Through this act the proletariat liberates the means of production from their previous capitalist encumbrance, giving its socialized character freedom to succeed.

Social production following a preciously set-up plan will now be possible. The development of production makes the further existence of various social classes anachronistic. To the degree that class production disappears, the political power of the state will die away. Men, finally the masters of their own kind of socialization, become thereby also the masters of nature, masters over themselves.[224]

A similar outline for the future was given by Engels in his "Anti-Duehring" when he referred to the necessity of transforming the old mode of production from the bottom up.

Whereas work had previously meant a form of slavery, it would now become a means of liberation for man, offering to each the opportunity to utilize his mental and physical talents. Greater productivity, already in evidence under capitalism, would expand immensely under socialization. No return to the pre-technology

50

era and to the old division of labor could be contemplated, and large-scale industry would remain in existence, as would the need for changes in the function and general flexibility of labor.[225] Socialism would provide for long-range economic planning for the benefit of the whole community. The contrast between city and country would thus be removed, along with local bottlenecks of the productive centers, cut off from the raw materials as they had been under capitalism. In brief, the old economic division of labor would be revolutionized with the seizure of all the means of production in the course of the social revolution. Instead of a division of labor, there would be an organization of production in which all would participate, and from which all would benefit.[226] The failure of the Revolution of 1848 indicated to Engels that the proletariat was still far from the goal of gaining a victory "in one great blow" and instead had to move forward slowly but steadily from position to position. Although it had failed, Engels gave credit to the Revolution for bequeathing to the international proletariat a revolutionary heritage.[227] In another passage in the same source, Engels wrote that the time of revolution by small and determined minorities at the head of "unconscious" masses had passed forever.[228] The implication was that the successful revolution would be a mass revolution, fought by and for the masses themselves.

Few references exist in Engels' writing as to whether the communist revolution would come about in one country or simultaneously in a number of countries. In his "Principles of Communism" ("Grundsaetze des Kommunismus") Engels clearly denied that the revolution could take place in one country only. He explained his position in terms of the existing interdependence of all nations, created by modern industry and trade, and the fact that in all civilized states a similar split between bourgeoisie and proletariat had come about. The revolution therefore would occur more or less simultaneously in more than one state, at least in England, the United States, France and Germany. It would develop faster or slower in a given state depending on the industrialization, wealth and productive forces. Engels presumed that it would be fastest in England and slowest in Germany. But it would affect

51

all other states as well and would therefore be a truly universal revolution.[229] A similar reference is found in his "German Ideology," in which Engels wrote that the universal phenomena of the propertyless masses would affect all states by revolutionary changes in other states. Communism, he said, could not exist in a locality, but could succeed only "at once and simultaneously." It all tied in with the universal development of production and the international exchange of production with which it was linked together.[230]

Although Engels repeatedly stated that in all probability the social revolution would begin in England, he did not dismiss other possibilities. But, in his "Social Conditions in Russia" ("Soziales aus Russland") he attacked as erroneous the speculations of a Russian revolutionary critic, Peter Tkachov, who had claimed the social revolution could occur more easily in Russia than in Western Europe. Engels' argument was that modern socialism presupposed the existence of a bourgeois class and resulting class conflicts, as well as a highly developed social productivity. Neither factor existed in Russia at that time.[231] From Engels' point of view, Tkachov was, therefore, ignorant of the premise upon which socialism was built. He also contested Tkachov's notion that Russia was the "chosen people" of socialism.[232] However, he was willing to consider the possibility of a Russian revolution in view of the decomposition of Russia's society and the break-up of communal ownership *without* having to go through the same stages as Western Europe, provided such a revolution was the signal for a revolution of the *West,* so that both would supplement each other.[233] In a letter from London on April 23, 1885, to Vera J. Zasulich, a Russian socialist and one of the founders of the first Marxist groups in the Russian workers' movement, Engels admitted that the Russians were approaching "their 1789." "The revolution *must* break out there in a given time; it *may* break out there any day." [234] In a similar letter on February 24, 1893, also from London to Nicolai Danielson, a Russian economist and translator of *Das Kapital,* Engels himself furnished the explanation on why Russian peasantry might be able to "skip" the "usual" intermediate

52

bourgeois stages: "No doubt the commune and to a certain extent the artel, contained germs which under certain conditions might have developed and saved Russia the necessity of passing through the torments of the capitalist regime." [235] Thus Engels recognized at least the possibility of a Russian revolutionary future based on its experience with communal ownership which needed only to be more fully collectivized and transformed into a higher form to serve as a starting point for a communist development, provided it were supported by a successful proletarian revolution carried out in Western Europe.[236]

CHAPTER V
ANARCHISM VERSUS THE
PROLETARIAN DICTATORSHIP
AND THE ROAD TO THE
CLASSLESS COMMUNIST SOCIETY

Once the social revolution had broken out, what degree of governmental control was to be expected from the new regime? To look for immediate anarchistic elimination of the authoritarian state as the first act of the revolutionary government would be totally absurd. As Engels had freely acknowledged in his article, "On Authority," "A revolution is certainly the most authoritarian thing that exists."[237] As an example, Engels pointed to the Parisian Commune, which could not have lasted a single day without authoritarianism; it would, in fact, probably have lasted longer had more authoritarianism been employed. Any other way of looking at this matter was, according to Engels, treasonable to the proletarian revolution.[238]

At this point, it would perhaps be advisable to investigate further the relationship between anarchism and proletarian authoritarian statism. *Marx's Critique of the Gotha Program* (*Kritik des Gothaer Programms*), which is an analysis of the progressive stages of communist society written in 1875, declared that the period of revolutionary transformation from the capitalist to the communist society coincided with a political transitional period in which the state could be nothing but the revolutionary dictatorship of the proletariat. According to Marx, a communist society did not develop "on its own foundations, but, on the contrary, emerged from capitalist society, and was therefore in every respect, economically, morally, and intellectually, still stamped with the birthmarks of the old society from whose womb it had emerged."[239] Communism, then, for Marx and Engels, was the highest phase in this evolving process. It was only at this final stage that state and law would cease to function. Similar ideas were expressed in the "German Ideology" and in Engels' "Anti-Duehring," to which we shall return later.

While communism taught that the state was a necessity only so long as antagonistic classes existed, and that the state and legal system were conditioned by the existence of classes, anarchists, such as Michael Bakunin, were advocating the immediate abolition of the state and its machinery as soon as the social revolution had occurred. Bakunian anarchism thus denied that the state had any need for a period of transition, even if that transitional period took the form of a dictatorship of the proletariat. Any form of authority, even that of the proletarian, was for them an evil that had to be abolished.[240]

Marx's and Engels' writings dealt sufficiently with the problem of the conquest of the bourgeois state by the proletariat, and some information is also available, as we have shown, on the future proletarian state. Little was written, however, on the last and decisive phase of communism, the transition from the proletarian state to the stateless society. What scanty information exists is found almost exclusively in Engels. Two of his polemic essays, written in 1872/73 against the Bakunian anarchism in the Italian journal La Plebe, clearly distinguished between anarchism and communism: the former wanted to abolish the political state all at once, while in the latter, the political state, in the form of the dictatorship of the proletariat, would disappear only gradually, in accordance with the materialist conception of history.[241] However, the ultimate form of communism, whether coming sooner as the Bakunists envisioned the very first phase, or later, as Marx and Engels pictured the gradual dissolution, would be one of anarchism.

Some scholars have claimed that Engels' "postponed" anarchism would hardly seem to justify any valid distinction between communism and Bakunism.[242] Engels would have contested such an interpretation, which, in effect, equated anarchism with Marxism. In fact, Engels wrote to Bernstein on January 28, 1884, defending himself against the allegation that he had made concessions to the anarchists.[243] So far as the originality of the idea of anarchism was concerned, Engels pointed out, he and Marx had written about the destruction of the state authority before anarchists ever existed, and gave as evidence two quotations, one from "The Poverty of Philosophy:"

As it develops, the working class will substitute for the old civil society an association which will exclude classes and their antagonism and there will be no more political power—properly so-called—since political power is an exact official summary of the antagonisms in civil society.[244]

The other quotation was from *The Communist Manifesto:*

When in the course of development class distinctions have disappeared . . . the public power will lose its political character. Political power so-called is merely the organized force of one class for oppressing another.

Engels' clearest formulation of proletarian authoritarianism, as distinguished from anarchism of the Bakunian brand, is contained in his essay "On Authority." [245] It is pointed out that the term "authoritarianism" had been misunderstood, if not deliberately abused. All modern industrial and agricultural economics, he wrote, have tended to replace "isolated" action with "combined" action of individuals; large-scale industry and large-scale agriculture required large-scale organization. Organization, in turn, was impossible without authority. Should capitalism be dethroned as the result of a social revolution, if the toilers had become the collective owners of all industrial property and land, how could anti-authoritarians reason that all authority must disappear?

Furthermore, by examining the changes in the cotton mills, railroads and shipping industries, Engels observed that the modern means of production and circulation had vastly expanded, and with this expansion had come increase in the realm of authority. He did expect, however, that the political authoritarian state would disappear in the ultimate course of the social revolution, meaning, as he explained, that public functions would lose their political character and be transformed into "simple administrative functions" which would take care of the "true social interest." This was a process, he stated, concerning which all socialists could agree. But, he insisted, it was not possible to abolish the political state all at once, even before the removal

56

of the social conditions out of which the bourgeois state had grown.[246] In his article on "The Bakunists at Work," *Volksstaat,* October 31, 1873, analyzing the failure of Bakunists in the Spanish rebellion during the summer of 1873, Engels ridiculed the clash of reality with the "ultrarevolutionary" slogans of anarchy.[247]

Engels considered the immediate abolition of all authority to be objectionable. Equally objectionable was Bakunin's plan to order a strike in Spain as a means of starting the social revolution in which all workers of a state or even of the entire world would go on strike simultaneously, in order to force the propertied classes to surrender.[248]

Engels judged the Spanish anarchistic movement to be a failure on a number of different scores. First, the Bakunists were forced to discard all their original programs as soon as they were actually faced with a serious revolutionary liberation. Second, their anarchy did not abolish the state but created many new small states. Third, the workers did not hesitate to participate in the petty-bourgeois movement instead of carrying out their revolution on their own strength. Fourth, the masses had joined the rebellion without any definite program and without knowing what they really wanted. Thus Engels concluded that the rebellion had been doomed to failure even before it started. "All that was left of the principles of anarchy, of the free federation of independent groups, etc., was a boundless and senseless division into fragments of the revolutionary means of battle," which made it possible for a handful of government troops to quell the rebellion. The Bakunists in Spain had taught a lesson of how a revolution ought *not* to be conducted.[249]

Other contrasts between anarchism and communism were suggested in Engels' letter of January 24, 1872, to Theodor Cuno, a German socialist who supported Marx during the Hague Congress of the First International in 1872. The letter stated that the anarchist:

does not regard capital, i.e., the class antagonism between capitalists and wage workers which has arisen through social development, but the *state* as the main evil to be abolished. While the great mass of the social-democratic workers hold our view that the state power is nothing more than the organization which the ruling classes—landowners and capitalists—have provided for themselves in order to protect their social privileges, Bakunin maintains that it is the *state* which has created capital, that the capitalist has his capital *only by the grace of the state.* As, therefore, the state is the chief evil, it is above all the state which must be done away with, and then capitalism will go to blazes of itself. We, on the contrary, say: Do away with capital, the concentration of all means of production in the hands of the few and the state will fall of itself. The difference is an essential one: without a previous social revolution the abolition of the state is nonsense; the abolition of capital *is* precisely the social revolution, and involves a change in the whole mode of production.[250]

And again, on April 18, 1883, Engels wrote from London to Philipp Van Patten, Secretary of the Central Labor Union in New York:

> Since 1845 Marx and I have held the view that *one* of the ultimate results of the future proletarian revolution will be the gradual dissolution of the political organization known by the name of *state* . . . with the disappearance of an exclusively wealth-possessing minority there also disappears the necessity for the power of armed oppression, or state power. At the same time, however, it was always our view that in order to attain this and the other far more important aims of the future social revolution, the working class must first take possession of the organized political power of the state and by its aid crush the resistance of the capitalist class and organize society anew.[251]

It is clear, therefore, that for Engels, the organization of the state had to continue after the proletarian revolution had destroyed the bourgeois state. The state would, of course, have to be considerably altered in order to retain its newly conquered power. Like any other political organization, the proletarian state would have to secure its position by oppression of its opponents. The major difference from the past would be, however, that for the first time, the state would be in the hands of a majority of the people.[252]

The characterizing of the state as a class-state was strongly and repeatedly emphasized throughout Engels' writings, by which he disassociated himself clearly from Hegel's idealized concept of the state standing above the classes. For instance, in "The Origin of the Family, of Private Property and of the State," Engels rejected the notion that the state was, as Hegel had asserted, the "realization of the spiritual ideal," "the picture and realization of reason." Instead, the state has always been the product of a given society at a given stage of economic development, which implied for Engels the existence of conflicting class interests within the state. One of the main functions of the state was exactly that of keeping the opposing class in check and therefore of developing into a foreign element poised against the checked and restrained class. As a rule the state has been the political enemy of the suppressed class.[253]

Not only did Engels reject Hegel's idealization of the state, but he also claimed that historically speaking, it had not existed in the very remotest times and need not exist in the future, either. The following passage is perhaps the most frequently quoted one of Engels' writings on this problem:

The state has (therefore) not been in existence from all eternity. Societies has existed which got along without it, having no idea of the state and state authority. At a certain level of economic development, related by necessity to the division of the society into classes, the state became a necessity because of this division. We are now rapidly approaching a stage in the development of production in which the need for classes has not only ceased to exist, but has become a positive hindrance to production. They will fall as inevitably as they came into existence originally. With them inevitably falls the state. The society which newly organizes production on the basis of a free and equal association of the producers will put the whole machinery of the state where it belongs: into the museum of antiquities, next to the spinning wheel and the bronze axe.[254]

Another reference to the class character of the state is contained in Engels' "Ludwig Feuerbach." The state is described there as an organ protecting security of society against attacks from internal and external enemies. The ruling class, however, has taken over the state and has come to operate as an autonomous institution within the society, thus ceasing to function on behalf of the whole community. Ultimately the ruling class in any class-state becomes the monopolistic element within the state, using it for its special security, benefit and perpetuation of class interests.[255] The state has been largely conditioned by the "changing needs of the . . . society, by the supremacy of this or that class, in the last instance, by the development of the productive forces and the conditions of exchange." Engels declared this to have been the case at all times, whether it was the ancient state in which slave owners used the state as an instrument of suppressing the slaves, the feudal state which served the nobility by keeping down the serfs, or the bourgeois, democratic capitalist state with its system of wage-earning and exploitation.[256] In the "German Ideology" too, Engels warned against overestimating the value of the state as an institution for the general welfare of all its citizens, which he called an illusion. Division of labor had created separate classes and class interests, and the state had become the arena in which the resulting class conflicts were fought out. Battles between democracy, aristocracy and monarchy, battles for extension of the suffrage, etc., have been merely the outward appearances of actually existing battles between classes.[257] All institutions, constitutions and laws of the state have been based on class distinctions and could never claim to rest on the "free will" of all citizens.[258]

The practical conclusion which Engels drew from his concept of the class nature of the state was the conviction that the proletarian state could not continue on the basis of the defunct bourgeois state. The workers must for their own survival destroy the old machinery which had been employed against them. As the bourgeois state had become the power of safeguarding the special interests of the capitalists, so the proletarians must transform the state to suit their own special interests. The philosophical conception of the state as God's kingdom on earth, founded on eternal truth and justice with the ensuing veneration of the state and all its paraphernalia was plain nonsense. Engels wrote on the occasion of the twentieth anniversary of the Parisian Commune, March 18, 1891,

> In reality the state is nothing more than a machine for the suppression of one class by another . . . and in the best of cases an evil which was inherited by the proletariat, the victor in the battle for class domination . . . and which it must curtail possibly, at once, until a new generation raised under new and free conditions of society will be able to do away with the whole trash of state (*Staatsplunder*).[259]

When the point is reached of doing away with the "whole trash of state," the meeting of minds between communists and anarchists would be finally established, as we have noted before. Compared to the impetuous anarchists, the communists, and among them most significantly, Engels himself, seemed to be almost procrastinators or evolutionaries. Communism, then, was a final stage to be reached after many intermediary and gradual stages. In one of his writings Engels listed twelve successive stages, which can be summarized briefly as follows:

1. Limitation of private property through vexatious, burdensome taxes;
2. Gradual expropriation of all property;
3. Confiscation of property of all emigrants and rebels;
4. Reorganization of labor with the intent of abolishing the competition of workers among themselves;
5. Introduction of universal and compulsory duty of labor;
6. Centralization and nationalization of credit and the monetary system;
7. Expansion of the means of production;
8. National education of all children;
9. Establishment of communal housing projects;
10. Destruction of inferior houses and city sections;
11. Equalization of inheritance rights for illegitimate and legitimate children;
12. Concentration and nationalization of all means of transportation.[260]

The theory of the gradualness with which Engels envisaged the social revolution proceedings, corresponded to the gradualness with which he anticipated the political state's disappearance. This thought was expressed in a number of his writings, as, for instance, in his letter to Bebel written between March 18 and 28, 1875, Engels postulated that with the introduction of the new social order, the state would dissolve itself and finally disappear completely. The state was, only a transitional institution (*voruebergehende Einrichtung*) acting in the interest of the revolution, chiefly keeping down its adversaries.

Parenthetically it ought to be mentioned here that Lenin considered this part of Engels' letter to Bebel "the most remarkable observation in the works of Marx and Engels on the state."[261] Like Engels, Lenin anticipated the disappearance of the state. He followed Engels' explanation for the inevitable decline of democracy under the impact of socialism: "If we are not to mock at common sense and history, then clearly we cannot speak of 'pure democracy' so long as different *classes* exist, but we can speak only of *class* democracy."[262] Classlessness, Lenin implied, would end the usefulness of democracy, as well as of any other form of government. As he wrote, "We establish as our final aid the liquidation of the state, i.e., of any sort of organized and systematic constraint, of all coercion of human beings in general."[263] Another agreement with Engels' theories on the withering of the state is contained in Lenin's speech given in May 1918, in which he said that "the nearer we come to the establishment of a socialist system, the less necessity there is for a purely administrative apparatus . . . that apparatus of the old state is doomed to die."[264]

According to Engels, after the proletariat had seized the state and transformed the means of production into communal property, the proletariat would liquidate itself as a separate class.[265] With the elimination of all class distinctions and contrasts, the state would be cancelled out, too. The state, by becoming at last the representative of all classes, would thereby become superfluous in one area after the other and the state would "go to sleep by itself." [266] The state would not be "abolished" but would "wither away." [267]

We shall quote now in full this classical statement on the gradual disappearance of the state at the threshold of communist anarchy, as contained in Engels' "Anti-Duehring," as well as in his "The Development" with only minor differences of style between them:

Whilst the capitalist mode of production more and more completely transforms the great majority of the population into proletarians, it creates the power which, under penalty of its own destruction, is forced to accomplish this revolution. Whilst it forces on more and more the transformation of the vast means of production, already socialized, into state property, it shows itself the way to accomplishing this revolution. *The proletariat seizes political power and turns the means of production in the first instance into state property.* But in doing this, it abolishes itself as proletariat, abolishes also the state as state. Society thus far, based upon class antagonisms, had need of the state, that is, of an organization of the particular class, which was *pro tempore* the exploiting class, for the maintenance of its external conditions of production, and, therefore, especially, for the purpose of forcibly keeping the exploited classes in the condition of oppression corresponding with the given mode of production (slavery, serfdom, wage-labour). The state was the official representative of society as a whole, the gathering of it together into a visible embodiment. But it was this only in so far as it was the state of that class which itself represented, for the time being, society as a whole: in ancient times, the state of slave-owning citizens; in the Middle Ages, the feudal lords; in our own time, the bourgeoisie. When at last it becomes the real representative of the whole society, it renders itself unnecessary. As soon as there is no longer any social class to be held in subjection; as soon as class rule, and the individual struggle for existence based upon our present anarchy in production, with the collisions and excesses arising from these, are removed, nothing more remains to be repressed, and a special repressive force, a state, is no longer necessary. The first act by virtue of which the state really constitutes itself the representative of the whole society—the taking possession of the means of production in the name of society—that is, at the same time, its last independent act as a state. State interference in social relations becomes, in one domain after another, superfluous, and then withers away of itself; the government of persons is replaced by the administration of things, and by the conduct of processes, of production. The state is not "abolished." *It withers away.*[268]

For Engels, classlessness led to statelessness, as we have shown. The notion that the proletarian state, might have to continue operating in defense of the socialist fatherland, even after classlessness had been largely accomplished, because of the "danger" of attacks from the 'encircling" capitalist states, had not yet been anticipated.[269]

Because of the causal relationship between class and state, Engels' views on classes requires some amplification. In the "German Ideology," which, in spite of its great quantity of theoretical material, did not find a publisher in Marx's and Engels' times, the thesis of the seizure of political power by the proletariat as a phase toward classlessness was set up for the first time. The "German Ideology" was the joint product of Marx and Engels who agreed to write it in Brussels in the spring of 1845 as a form of critique of post-Hegelian German philosophy.[270]

One of the main themes of the "German Ideology" dealt with the impact of the ruling class in every epoch on all material and nonmaterial things; the ideological thoughts being subordinated to the material in accordance with the materialist conception of history.[271]

Similarly Engels expressed his views that all history had been a history of class war and that the antagonistic classes of a society had always been the results of the means of production and exchange, in a word, of the changing economic conditions of their epoch.[272] The task of the socialists, wrote Engels, was not to discover and develop a picture of a perfect society, but to delve into the economic circumstances which conditioned the conflict of the classes and to find the appropriate solution to the problem.[273]

No question existed in Engels' mind that peaceful coexistence of classes could ever work out satisfactorily. In every epoch, reasoned Engels, there was room for one dominant class only, which because of its exclusive power, was in a position to lead the entire nation. No progress and leadership could be expected except under the rule of a single class.[274]

Historically Engels felt that classes developed as soon as a given society had reached a stage in its civilization where a form of production and exchange was taking place, and as soon as an unequal distribution of products (as distinguished from primitive tribal or village communities with a more or less equal distribution) prevailed. With the differences in the distribution, class differences would begin to appear. The society would split up into the privileged and underprivileged, exploiting and exploited, ruling and ruled classes.[275] In a primitive society there might still be a certain equality, or at least, an absence of a social class. Common affairs were handled by common action or under the supervision of the community. With the growth of productive forces, however, new divisions of labor and, with them, organizations for securing separate interests had evolved. These tended to become autonomous and ended up with the perpetuation of their offices and positions vis-a-vis the bulk of society. In short, the class had come into existence.[276] The origin of classes which began with the division of the productive process and the unequal distribution of products could be traced as far back as the first clash of classes recorded in history, i.e., the antagonism of husband and wife in monogamy, the wife being the first "victim" of class oppression. Monogamy, for Engels, was the original cell of civilized society in which class contrasts and conflicts could be studied first hand.[277]

If in the past the clashes had been conditioned by the division of labor which, in turn, was conditioned by the modes of production and exchange, Engels concluded that, by a communist revolutionary overthrow of the existing society, the division of labor would also be transformed and the separateness and antagonistic nature of classes ended.[278] Engels' thesis of the abolition of the former division of labor was a consistently returning theme in his writings, as for instance when he wrote in his "Anti-Duehring" that the old means of production must be transformed from the bottom up and particularly the old division of labor must disappear. The time would arrive when no person or group could shrug off its responsibility to participate in productive work along with the class of the oppressed toilers. With compulsory participation of all in labor, the distinction between masters and servants would cease to exist. All men would then be able to advance their physical and mental abilities.[279] In fact, asserted Engels, this process was already in operation under capitalism itself, as witnessed by the mechanization and the ensuing expansion of production and productivity. The establishment of large trusts and corporations served to overcome the obstacles and wastes of the less technologically developed and localized industries, and constantly changing methods had come to modify the functions and processes of labor.[280] Capitalism itself had come to realize the truth of what Marx had called in *Das Kapital* the disaster of the "anarchy in society."[281]

With the abolition of private property, explained Engels in his "Principles of Communism," society would take over all the means of production, transportation, exchange and distribution from the previous owners and all products would be administered in accordance with a planned economy. Economic crises would disappear, as would overproduction. All needs would be satisfied. General progress would set in. Industry and agriculture would expand. All production would be changed with far-reaching consequences for the producers themselves. Division of labor would end and with it division into classes. The workers would cease to be deliberately deprived of understanding and of participating in the total process of production, chained as they had been in the past to one small segment of the productive process during capitalism. They would be enabled to develop their talents and to move from one branch and skill to another, which would eliminate deadening monotony of work. The difference of industrial and agricultural work, and therefore the difference between city and country class, would also end.[282] For the first time in history, Engels claimed, through rational division of labors all members of society would be in possession of abundant means and would at last find sufficient leisure to be able to devote themselves to education, the arts and sciences.

These would therefore cease to be monopolized by the ruling classes. With the transformation of production by communism, all pretexts for the continued existence of a ruling class would terminate. In fact, as a result of the industrial revolution of the last hundred years, all justification for a ruling class had been struck at the roots. And so much the better. The existence of a ruling class had increasingly become an obstacle in the development of industrial production, and also of the arts and sciences.[283]

CHAPTER VI

THE COMMUNIST SOCIETY,
A BLUEPRINT FOR THE FUTURE

There is no lack of material in Engels' writings on the future of the communist society. Piecing together from various sources the most important of his conceptions about the nature of this future society would result in a version with the following attributes:

According to Engels, the *interests* of the individuals composing this future society will be united and will coincide with the interests of the *community*. Competition will be abolished. No contrast between rich and poor, no inequality in the distribution of the necessary things of life will exist. Enrichment of the individual based upon the impoverishment of others will end. Production will be regulated according to needs. Production, as well as consumption, will be planned in an orderly system.[284] "Irrational" and "impractical" economics will be avoided. Aggressive wars, in which the workers fight for an "imaginary fatherland," will end and also the waste of manpower in non-productive standing armies.[285] All other forms of unproductive labor, such as the services rendered to the wealthy by servants, drivers and cooks, will cease. Unemployment and forced idleness will be eliminated, and, with it, prostitution, begging, loitering and degrading work generally.[286]

With the end of private property, crimes against property will end. Other crimes will be drastically reduced because people will not be exposed any further to gross social discriminations. Civil litigation will become of minor significance. All matters of administration, related to law enforcement and the meting out of justice will become virtually superfluous.[287] Production will not be reduced nor returned to the pre-machine age. No retrogression to a feudal or guild-age will be permitted to take place. On the contrary, industry will be geared to large-scale and ultimately world-wide productive proportions.[288]

With the end of the division of labor, the individual will be enabled to develop his talents and preferences fully.[289] Instead of being separated by class barriers, all individuals, will participate in constructive work as individuals, not as members of a class but in the name of the communist society. Only under communism will personal freedom assume meaningfulness: It will cease to be enjoyed only by the members of a select class.[290] The communist society will provide for a plan of production in which all its members will participate, not in competition but as members of an association. Economic planning and the central direction of all labor forces will lead to cutting down of the number of working hours the individual is expected to put in.[291] Community housing projects will be carried out similar to those proposed by the utopian socialist Robert Owen, involving the construction of large blocks of houses in place of single and ill-planned houses in villages and towns.[292] Community housing will be accompanied by other community activities, such as dining in communal places. This will end the waste of material, heating, fuel, gas and other necessities of the presently existing "split-economy." [293]

Each individual worker will be guaranteed the full reward of his labor, i.e., the "entire existing society of laborers will be the collective owner of all products of its labor. Its fruits will be distributed in part for the consumption of its members, partly for replacement and improvement of its means of production, and partly for a reserve fund for later production and consumption." [294] Physical, as well as class, differences between city and country will be erased, as the big industrial cities will end with the end of the capitalist modes of production.[295] Ultimately each worker will have his own homestead, but in the meantime will stay in houses expropriated from bourgeois owners. Workers will be billeted in the towns by rationally redistributing the population. The miserable and unsanitary slum sections of the workers will be destroyed.[296]

The family will finally become a truly private relationship in which society cannot intervene. This can be accomplished by eliminating private property and by providing common public education for all children which will thereby abolish dependencies of spouses on their husbands and of children upon their parents. Engels denied all propagandist talk of the community of women under communism, holding that immorality, prostitution, etc., were by-products of capitalism. Whatever community of women had existed had been under the capitalist not communist system.[297] On this point, Engels identified himself with Marx who, in *Das Kapital*, had pointed out the destruction of the workers' family under capitalism and had appealed for a "higher form" of the family and improved relationships between the sexes.[298] Like the utopian socialists, Engels advocated socialization of production and extended socialization to the education of youth.[299]

Evidently there was no room for religion in Engels' future communist society. What, then, was to take its place? Engels was the most vociferous among the Young Hegelians, who professed atheism, as he rejected all forms of mysticism and metaphysics. This profession probably reflected the influence of Ludwig Feuerbach's *The Essence of Christianity (Das Wesen des Christentums)* with its strong materialist approach toward religion.[300] Yet Engels' own words indicated that he did not want to be labeled a "pure" atheist. For instance, in his letter to Bernstein in the late summer of 1884, Engels disassociated himself from atheism because it was, as he said, only a "negation" of religion and, at the same time, itself becoming a religion by always making reference to religion.[301] In "The Position in England," Engels admitted that communists, too, felt the inner vacuum, the spiritual emptiness and untruthfulness of their times.[302] But what Engels advocated was not a return to "conventional" religion, based on a concept of the "divine," but a "human" religion. "We want to abolish all that is supernatural and superhuman . . . The pretense . . . of being superhuman and supernatural is the root of all insincerity and lie." [303] If this approach to religion made him an atheist, Engels added, so let it be.

More specifically, Engels accused Christians of disregarding humanity, of withholding reality from secular history, and of beguiling men by an "other-worldly, abstract, and even fictitious and legendary history." Religion based on Christ was "wild nonsense and absolutely without substance." Instead of divinely revealed history, Engels' religion celebrated human content.[304] Faith in the progress of man, in victory over irrationality, in battling successfully with nature to promote better and moral conditions of life, these alone were worthy to be believed in, in place of recourse to an abstract God.[305] "Who was God?" Engels asked rhetorically: "God is Man." Man had only to recognize himself, to measure all things of life by his own standard and to seek to establish a truly human world according to the demands of his own nature. God dwelt in man's own chest, not in an imaginary other-worldly non-existing region beyond time and space.[306] No other salvation existed for man to escape from emptiness and unsteadiness than to wipe out all religious hallucinations and to return to man himself, instead of to God.[307] It was of no relevance, wrote Engels in 1843, that a few passages in the Bible spoke of some of the early Christians as living in a relationship of joint property. The general spirit of the Bible, and that was all that counted, ran counter to the principle of communism.[308]

In his introduction to the English edition of "Socialism Utopian and Scientific," published in 1892, Engels contrasted the "religious bigotry" of the English "respectable middle class" with his materialism or at least with "very advanced freethinking" following the general trend of the continental religious scepticism. Agnosticism was nothing but a form of materialism, wrote Engels; both denied intervention from without. There was no room for a divine creator.

In Kant's time, our knowledge of natural objects was indeed so fragmentary that he might well suspect, behind the little we knew about each of them, a mysterious thing-in-itself. But one after another of these elusive things have been grasped, analyzed, and, what is more, *reproduced* by the giant progress of science, and what we can produce we certainly cannot consider as unknowable.. (Man) as

71

far as he is a scientific man, as far as he *knows* anything, (he) is a materialist; outside his science, in spheres
about which he knows nothing, he translates his ignorance
into Greek and calls it agnosticism.[309]

It matters little whether Engels should be classified as an
atheist, agnostic, or materialist. He was convinced that proletarians were the natural opponents of religion. Yet atheism
pure and simple was somewhat out of date: "They (men) are
simply through with God. They live and think in a real world
and are therefore materialists."[310]

Consistently with his materialist conception, Engels asserted
that religion was determined economically, although he admitted
that religion was the furthest removed from materialist life.
Religion developed like any other ideology, i.e., in relationship
to existing material conditions. Comparative mythology, Engels
asserted, has proved that original religious beliefs were shaped
by existing class conditions of given ethnic groups. Once
formed religion has tended to become conservative in tradition
and its economic origin has been forgotten.[311]

It was the bourgeoisie, not the proletariat, which had actually
destroyed religion. The *Communist Manifesto* stated this quite
clearly:

> The (bourgeoisie) has drowned the most heavenly ecsta-
> sies of religious fervor, of chivalrous enthusiasm, of Phili-
> stine sentimentalism in the icy water of egotistical calcula-
> tion . . . (For) exploitation, veiled by religious and politi-
> cal illusions, it has substituted naked, shameless, direct, brutal
> exploitation. The bourgeoisie has stripped of its halo every
> occupation hitherto honored and looked upon with reverent
> awe.[312]

The proletarian, Engels reasoned, was bound to be against
religion: He was more humanitarian than the bourgeois and,
therefore, less in need of religious sublimation. Because of his
insufficient education, the proletarian was less doctrinaire and
less prejudiced in religious matters. The proletarians' indifference to religion was not any more than that of the bourgeois;
although he pretended to be religiously zealous, he lived only
for *this* world.[313]

Engels distinguished indigenous or natural religion (*natur-wuechsig*), as for instance, fetishism of negroes, from artificial religion (*Kunstreligion*), that which had been manipulated and spoiled by the priests.[314] When the Roman Empire needed to impose its religion upon its subjected peoples, Christianity was its best device. It did not matter that it was a "nonsense-religion" (*Unsinnsreligion*): the end justified the means. Nor were the theologians disturbed by the thought that the Gospel was historically absolutely unprovable and that even the historical existence of Christ was a matter of doubt.[315]

Engels suggested that parallels could be drawn between the history of early Christianity and the modern working class movements. Christianity, too, had originally identified itself with the slaves, the poor and subjugated. The difference between Christianity and socialism, however, was that while the former preached salvation for man after death the latter placed emphasis on salvation in this world.[316] The objectionable feature of Christian otherworldliness, according to Engels, was precisely its disinterest in the need for transformation and improvement of society.

What did Engels hold for the future of religion in the communist society? The clearest answer to this matter is contained in his "Anti-Duehring."[317] Religion was explained there as nothing more than a "fantastic reflection" of external powers in the minds of men. These powers which dominated man's life were reflections by which worldly powers were transposed to supernatural ones. In man's remotest past, Engels explained, he was ruled by many supernatural powers. The more civilized man became, the more he came to recognize that societal, i.e., economic, in addition to supernatural powers, ruled over him. Mysterious supernatural powers gradually evolved into attributes of economic powers. At an advanced stage of development, the supernatural and economic attributes of religion became transferred from many gods to one single god, who still was only the abstract reflection of the economically-conditioned man. According to Engels, man had been conditioned, whether he realized it or not, during polytheism as well as monotheism, by the reflection on his economic environment. Thus, in the bourgeois society, man was conditioned by bourgeois economics, and this conditioning was reflected in his religious beliefs. However, after the bourgeoisie would be overthrown and all means of production collectivized, man would not only *think* for himself, but would also *direct* himself and liberate himself from "alien" means of production which hitherto had ruled over him. The moment would then come, Engels predicted, when the last power which had dominated men economically and religiously would disappear and with it *all* religious reflection, "simply because there was nothing further to be reflected." Like the bourgeois state, bourgeois religion would die a natural death; it would wither away.[318]

In "The Development" Engels expounded economic theories which were intended to show the historical necessity of the advent of socialism.[319] The bourgeoisie, he pointed out, owed its rise and progress to victory over localism and guildism. As the capitalist economy advanced, it would encounter the same kind of formidable opposition in the proletariat as, in former times, feudalism had met in the bourgeoisie. The communist economy, in turn, would become heir to the bourgeois economy.

Economic evolution, in each of its stages, was subject to changes in the modes of production, (*Produktionsverhaeltnisse*). It began with a system of production by crafts—and guild-merchants and peasants, in which, although limited and hardly lucrative, all means of production normally belonged to the producers themselves.

Capitalism, on the contrary, operated by forcing first the concentration of the local means of production, and then later the expansion of the means of production, as Marx had described in great detail in the fourth chapter of *Das Kapital*.[320] Engels wanted to emphasize the fact that, during the Middle Ages, the end product had belonged to the single producer, i.e., that one's personal labor earned one the reward of owning the goods one produced. The economic clashes of modern times resulted from the capitalist economics of production, which diminished the benefits of individual production drastically. The producers, i.e., the workers, became reduced to wage earners. The more concentration of the means of production in the hands of the capitalists, the larger the reduction of man to proletarianism.[321]

There was one development in this process which had not been anticipated by capitalism: in the end, production came to dominate the producers. The capitalist, producing for himself, without knowledge or understanding of how his production would affect the market and whether the demand would absorb the supply, found himself caught in the anarchy of his own economic system. As a result, the place of work became a veritable battlefield. Darwin's theory of the struggle for survival among biological species extended to the social scene.

Modern machines also contributed to the progressive dehumanization of the working class. It became a matter of economic necessity for capitalists to exploit their workers increasingly and to raise their productivity, while at the same time, reducing their wages to a bare minimum. The emergent dilemma for capitalists was that this tendency came to limit the consuming power of the masses considerably.[322] A similar picture was drawn by Marx, when he stated in *Das Kapital* that "accumulation of wealth at one pole is (therefore) at the same time accumulation of misery, agony of toil, slavery, ignorance, brutality and mental degradation at the opposite pole." [323]

Engels described the vicious circle of reduction in the volume of sales, available markets, and consumption, while the production of modern industrial goods continued to increase, causing a sharp discrepancy between markets and production. In the end, the bourgeois state, as the official representative of capitalist society, would have to take over the direction of all production. All private property would then be converted into state property. At this point, the bourgeoisie would have to admit that it was not indispensable in its past form.[324]

The newly transformed state, on becoming *the* capitalist in the state, would not thereby change its capitalist nature nor the conditions of the workingmen, nor would the state as national capitalist be in the position of finding an immediate solution for the capitalist crises. Economic crises and the conflict between capitalists and exploited citizens would come to an end only if, in place of the capitalist anarchy of production, economic planning were adopted, correlated to the needs of the entire community:

The solution can consist only in the practical recognition of the social nature of the modern forces of production, and therefore in the harmonizing of the modes of production, appropriation, and exchange through the socialized character of the means of production. And this can come about only by society openly and directly taking possession of the productive forces which have outgrown all control except that of society as a whole. The social character, both of the means of production and of the products themselves, today reacts against the producers, periodically disrupts all production and exchange, acts only like a law of nature working blindly, forcibly and destructively. But with the taking over by society of the productive forces, the social character of the means of production and of the products will be utilized by the producers with a perfect understanding of its nature, and instead of being a source of disturbance and periodic collapse, it will become the most powerful lever of production itself. . . . While the capitalist mode of production more and more completely transforms the great majority of population into proletarians, it creates the power which, under penalty of its own destruction, is forced to accomplish this revolution. While it forces on more and more the transformation of the vast means of production, already socialized, into state property, it shows itself the way to accomplishing this revolution. *The proletariat seizes political power and turns the means of production into state property.*[325]

There is more than one explanation for Engels' continual emphasis on the necessity of striving for a socialist society. Next in importance to the idea that wage-earning and capitalism resulted in conflicts and discrepancies inherent in the capitalist system was his theory that man had a right to a full and adequate economic existence. Under capitalism the system of private ownership of property, both in industry and agriculture, had denied this right to all who were not themselves proprietors of property.[326]

Whether in the form of interests, profits, rents or in any other form, the capitalist economy was based on what Engels called "immoral" enrichment, appropriation, and monopoly.[327] In Engels' *"Outlines for a Critique of National Economy,"* the "great waste" and inner contradictions of the capitalist economy were described: its overproduction and stagnation of work; its failure to develop and to utilize the highest productivity of land, capital, labor and science; its vacillating price system; its inhuman and destructive competition; and its "Malthusian blasphemy" against nature and mankind.[328]

Labor was the most important contributor to production and the source of all wealth, and yet it was exactly labor which was not fully compensated under the capitalist system. It was this reflection on the "unpaid" portion of labor which brought Engels to the same conclusion as that reached by Marx, through the same channels of reasoning, on the idea of marginal value (Mehrwert).[329]

There are several references in Engels writings concerning the economic theory of surplus or marginal value (which states that the workers receive only part of the value of their labor power, the difference between the wages and the full labor value (the "unpaid" labor) accruing instead to the capitalist). It was through the discovery of surplus value that the capitalist method of production, with the exploitation of the workers that occurs under capitalism and its inevitable downfall could be fully understood :[330]

"... Even if the capitalist purchases the working power of his laborer at its full value as a commodity on the market, he extracts still more value from it than he paid for it, and, in the ultimate analysis, this surplus value form those sums of value which add up to the constantly increasing masses of capital in the hands of the propertied classes. The genesis of capitalist production and the production of capital were both explained.[331]

A similar view was expressed in Engels' editorial in *The Labor Standard* of May 7, 1881 entitled "A Just Day's Wage for a Just Day's Work." Here Engels reiterated the theory of surplus value, namely, that the worker gave to the capitalist the full force of his labor, as much as he could give and still be able to repeat the same performance the next day. In exchange, he receives only as much as he needed to restore his strength to do another day's work. While the worker then gave a maximum, the capitalist paid only a minimum. The product of labor went to the capitalist, while the worker gained from it only the barest means of sustenance. A peculiar standard of justice, indeed! The editorial ended with an appeal to the workers to make themselves the owners of the means of production, raw materials, factories and machines.[332]

CHAPTER VII

PERSONAL PERFORMANCE, CO-OPERATION AND INTERACTION

Our study of Engels' theories on the difference between capitalist and socialist methods of production had indicated that his views were in conformity with those of Marx. In particular when he referred to the doctrine of surplus value, Engels acknowledged his indebtedness to Marx. For instance, when Engels commented on David Ricardo's original contribution to the study of the nature of surplus value, he wrote that Marx was much more thorough than Ricardo in the study and grasp of the impact of surplus value on labor and capital and, therefore, deserved the credit for making something out of it.[333] Again, after Engels had stated, in his essay, "On the Problem of Housing," that the idea of surplus value was the "cornerstone" of the capitalist method of production, he wrote, "Compare Marx's *Das Kapital* where this was first developed."[334] Even more explicitly, at the end of Part II of "The Development," Engels stated that Marx was responsible for "the two 'great discoveries,' the materialist conception of history and the revelation of the secret of capitalist production through the theory of surplus value." It was on the basis of these discoveries that socialism had become a science.[335]

It is not within the scope of this study to undertake a paragraph-by-paragraph textual comparison of the works of Marx and Engels (a Herculean task, indeed). Nevertheless in the case of the doctrine of surplus value and a few other areas, we want to examine the type of co-operation that existed between them, if for no other reason that to try to separate Engels' largely personal, individual conributions to socialist theories from his co-operative contributions.

The Communist Manifesto seems to us a fruitful target for examining the co-operation and interaction between Marx and Engels, as well as assessing the extent of Engels' personal performance. After Marx's death, Engels undertook to write a preface to the German edition of the Communist Manifesto in 1883. For Engels the fundamental, all-pervading proposition in the *Communist Manifesto* was that economic production and exchange and its resulting social structure in every epoch had been the foundation of the political and intellectual history of that period; that, consequently, the whole history of mankind had been one of class struggles, contests between exploiting and exploited, ruling and oppressed classes; that this struggle of classes had now reached a stage in which the exploited proletariat class could not attain its emancipation from the sway of the exploiting and ruling bourgeoisie without, at the same time, emancipating the entire society once and for all from all exploitation, oppression and class struggles.[336] "This fundamental proposition" Engels concluded, "belongs solely and exclusively to Marx."[337]

Yet, in Engels' own footnote to the same preface he noted, as he had in his preface to the English translation of 1888,[338] that "*we* had (underscoring ours) already been coming closer together (*genaehert*) on this fundamental proposition which was destined in my view to establish for the science of history the same progress that Darwin's theory of the science of nature had established, for several years before 1845. How far I had independently progressed (*voranbewegt*) toward it is best shown in my 'Position of the Working Class in England.' But when I met Marx at Brussels in the spring of 1845, he had already worked it out (*fertig ausgearbeitet*) and put it before me."[339]

The evidence would thus seem to indicate that while Engels was later most willing to bestow on Marx all the public credit for this explanation of the nature of the class struggle, he had himself evolved a fairly similar theory, for which he now also deserves recognition.

Furthermore, Engels and Marx were jointly and equally involved in reappraising the quality of and recommending changes in the *Communist Manifesto,* as indicated in their joint preface to the 1872 German edition. Although they both agreed as to the correctness of the general principles of the *Communist Manifesto,* they also saw need for changes in some details which the passage of twenty-five years had shown to be obsolete.[340]

It thus seems warranted that Engels' historical secondary position with respect to the Communist Manifesto must be reassessed. Marx was not the "sole and exclusive" originator of the proposition of the class struggle. Nor was the authorship of the *Manifesto* nearly so "joint" a project as has been supposed. Engels must be considered in more than one significant respect the leading guide in the initial formulation of the *Communist Manifesto* and even in the naming.

In September, 1847, the central organization of the Communist League in London sent a draft of a document called "Communist Confession of Faith" (*Kommunistisches Glaubensbekenntnis*) to the League's members in counties and towns. Because the draft's orientation toward utopian socialism, Marx and Engels, among others, refused to approve of it. A revised draft by Moses Hess which was prepared in Paris was criticized by the Parisian section of the Communist League on October 22. It was *Engels, not Marx,* who on that occasion criticized Hess' draft and who was commissioned to work on a new version. In Engels' letter to Marx on October 25-26, 1847, Engels described how he came to be commissioned: "Quite between ourselves, I have played a devilish trick on Mosi (Moses Hess). He had actually put through the most absurd revised confession of faith . . . I got myself commissioned to draft a new one . . . behind the backs of the communes."[341]

Engels' draft became known as the Principles of Communism. Commenting on his own draft, in a letter to Marx from Paris, November 23-24, 1847, Engels wrote:

I am bringing what I have done here with me; it is simply a narrative, but miserably put together in fearful haste. I begin: What is Communism? And then straight to the proletariat—history of its origin, difference from former work-

81

ers, development of the contradiction between proletariat and bourgeoisie, crises, results. . .[342]

Engels' outline of the Principles have, as can be seen by comparison, *the germs of the Communist Manifesto for which Engels himself considered the Principles to serve only as a preliminary sketch of a program.*[343]

We also want to point out that it was Engels, not Marx who attended the First Congress of the League at London in June, 1847, and who, in his capacity as a member, formulated the statement of principles for the reorganized League (which at that Congress changed its name from the League of the Just to Communist League):

> The purpose of the League is the overthrow of the bourgeoisie, the rule of the proletariat, the suppression of the old bourgeois society based as it was on contrasts of classes, and the establishment of a new society without classes and without private property.[344]

Engels even contributed to the choice of the name "Communist Manifesto": In the aforementioned letter to Marx of November 23-24, 1847, Engels stated, "I believe we had better drop the catechism form and call it 'Communist Manifesto.' As more or less history has got to be related in it, the form it has used hitherto is quite inadequate."[345] Similarly Engels wrote in his preface to the fourth German (1890) edition of the Communist Manifesto:

> We could not have called it a Socialist Manifesto. By 'socialist,' in 1847, was understood, on the one hand, the adherents of the various utopian systems: Owenites in England, Fourierists in France, both of them already reduced to the position of mere sects, and gradually dying out; on the other hand, the most multifarious social quacks, who, by all manners of tinkering, professed to redress, without any danger to capital and profit, all sorts of social grievances. In both cases, men outside the working-class had become convinced of the insufficiency of mere political revolutions and had proclaimed the necessity of a total social change; that portion then called itself "communist." It was a crude, rough-hewn, purely instinctive sort of communism;

still, it touched the cardinal point and was powerful enough among the working class to produce the utopian communism, in France of Cabet and in Germany of Weitling. Thus socialism was, in 1847, a middle-class movement; communism, a working-class movement. Socialism was, on the Continent at least, "respectable;" communism was the very opposite. And as our notion, from the very beginning, was that 'the emancipation of the working class must be the act of the working class itself,' there could be no doubt as to which of the two names we must take.[346]

There is no shortage of material in Engels' writings dealing with the substance of the *Communist Manifesto*. Not surprisingly, there are frequent references to the contrast and clashes of classes, the growing class-consciousness of the proletariat, and the destruction of the small producers.[347] Engels consistently repeated the idea that all conflicts had been class struggles and would remain so until all classes were abolished;[348] that all previously ruling classes had been small minorities, but that in modern history, the revolutions had become majority movements.[349] Principles underlying the *Communist Manifesto* were also contained in Engels' statements that the bourgeoisie had made itself the first class in politics and society that had unintentionally contributed to the advancement of the proletariat,[350] to the centralization of property and the destruction of the lower middle class,[351] the degrading of the vast majority of the people to the level of the proletariat,[352] the proletarization of the coalminers,[353] and the deepening and increasing frequency of economic crises.[354] The bourgeoisie was, therefore, responsible for the inevitability of violent solutions in view of the deeply rooted prejudice of the bourgeois class.[355]

Engels' deference to Marx and his overemphasis of his "weness" which seemed to disclaim much of his own contribution, can be balanced not only by his share in the preparation to the *Communist Manifesto,* but also by his *Ludwig Feuerbach and the End of Classical German Philosophy* which Friedrich Engels wrote shortly after April 1886, and in the preface of which he stated after Marx's death in February 21, 1888:

Since then (Marx's and Engels' joint study of the *Critique of Political Economy*) more than forty years have passed and Marx is dead without the opportunity for us to return to the subject matter (of Hegelian philosophy). So far as our relationship to Hegel is concerned, we expressed ourselves only occasionally but never in any comprehensive way.[356]

In his asterisk-footnote of the same preface (*Vorbemerkung*), Engels stated himself that he did not deny to have had a "certain independent" share in the elaboration of the theory.[357] Since, as has been indicated above, the *Ludwig Feuerbach,* etc., was Engels' significant analysis of Hegel's and Feuerbach's dialectic materialism (or dialectic idealism), Engels' statement in his own preface can serve as evidence that in less servile moments he was willing to admit that he contributed to a topic which was either insufficiently or not at all discussed with Marx and which, therefore, had to be completed, implemented or brought up to date by Engels himself.

Engels' works, we claim, such as the *Anti-Duehring, Ludwig Feuerbach and the End of Classical German Philosophy,* and his *Dialectics of Nature* were largely Engels' and not so much Marx's contributions, and dealt largely with Hegel's, Feuerbach's and Duehring's thoughts on dialectics, compared and contrasted Marx's and his own views on the subjects, as well as on the relationship between idealism, historical materialism and political economy. If one cannot consider Engels' work entirely "original," one must recognize, nonetheless, their most articulate quality as elaborations on classical Marxism. Furthermore, both the *Ludwig Feuerbach* and the *Dialectics of Nature* were published after Marx's death and include natural scientific data, not known to Marx in his lifetime. They introduced, as had been indicated in this study, new and empirical facts into the discussion and verification of dialectic materialism.

The *Anti-Duehring* itself, which was still published during Marx's lifetime some thirty years after the *German Ideology* of 1846, and which represents a major statement on classical Marxist philosophy, was essentially Engels' and not so much a joint product with Marx. Engels himself claimed that he had read the entire manuscript to Marx before it was to be printed, and the tenth chapter on economics ("From the Critical History") was written by Marx himself. Yet, in later years, in January 10, 1887, Engels explained himself the reasons why he and not Marx had assumed the work (written from 1876 to 1878): "Because of the division of labor which was arranged between Marx and myself, it became my task to represent our view in the periodical press, mainly in the battle with opposed views, in order that Marx could retain time for the elaboration of his great major work." [358] Although the contents and form of the *Anti-Duehring* was largely polemical, Engels asserted himself later in his letter to Eduard Bernstein of April 11, 1884, that his work became "an encyclopedic survey" of philosophical natural scientific and historical problems. [359] It should be noted also that on September 23, 1885, Engels in his "Prefaces to the Three Editions" of the *Anti-Duehring* wrote that his study against Duehring gave him "the opportunity of setting forth in a positive form *my views* (underscoring supplied) on controversial issues which are today of quite general scientific or practical interest." [360]   ,

Whether the *Anti-Duehring* was written with or without Marx's fully expressed approval (and there is no evidence that it was really given), it was Engels who presented an alternative system to Duehring's, a work which Lenin referred to as examining the "deepest problems of philosophy, of natural and societal science . . . an astoundingly comprehensive and instructive book," on which he (Lenin) based his *Materialism and Empirico-Criticism.* [361]

Three chapters of the *Anti-Duehring* were published with slight modifications in the form of a brochure, ("The Development of Socialism from Utopia to Science") to which this study has referred to on several occasions. The *Anti-Duehring* comprises much of Engels' knowledge in philosophy, economics, history, natural and military science. It did not only defend "orthodox" Marxism, but expanded and deepened it substantially. Much of it is an elaboration of Marxist theories.

Because of the importance of the *Anti-Duehring* and the fact that this study has drawn from it frequently, a brief summary may be in place here: The major focus of the *Anti-Duehring* is directed to the analysis of dialectic materialism which seems to permeate the entire work. Engels emphasizes the material unity of the world and the nexus between motion and material existence. It elevated dialectics to a center position among the laws of motion and development, of society and thought, pointing out the Marxist concept of the history of philosophical evolution. Engels demonstrates the operation of dialectic materialism in all the sciences, investigates the nature, rise and development of all life, the relationship between economics and politics, the place and nature of power in history, the rise of the classes and the class system, the problem of social equality, the origin and nature of the state, the relationship between morals and the law, the essence of religion and the material basis of military affairs.

In the sections on economics the *Anti-Duehring* defines and analyzes economics, pointing out its historical development and applies dialectics to Marx's theory of production, exchange and distribution of commodities. In the form of a broad outline of Marx's theories, Engels' *Anti-Duehring* emphasizes especially Marx's definition of value, labor, capital and marginal value. It characterizes the economic, political and intellectual weaknesses of the bourgeoisie, pointing out the conflict between the bourgeois regime and the increasing productivity which Engels sets into contrast with communist planned economy.

In the closing chapter Engels indicates dialectic materialism as an effective method to explore the capitalist modes of production and how historical materialism and the doctrine of the surplus (marginal) value forms the basis of scientific socialism, transferring socialism from a utopia to a science. The inevitable transition from capitalism to communism is pointed out, and the basic principles of the future communist society are outlined: the planned organization of production, the fullest development of productivity, the participation of all workers in the processing of their work, the elimination of the difference between physical and mental labor, between city and country; the abolition of all class distinctions, and with it the gradual withering away of the state; the replacement of governmental by societal organs, the changes in the family pattern and education, the disappearance of religion and the ultimate mastery of nature by man.

Any appraisal of Engels' full contribution to political thought would be imcomplete if his share in the completion and commentary of Marx' *Das Kapital* were omitted. As Engels stated in his preface to the third edition, November 7, 1883, it became his duty to take care of this edition and of the second volume bequeathed to him as a handwritten manuscript. As Engels pointed out, Marx himself had intended to reorganize the material of the first edition extensively, to add new material, and to implement it with more recent and statistical data. Because of his illness and his desire to complete his second volume, Marx had had to abandon that plan.[362] In his legacy Engels found a German copy of *Das Kapital* that was partly corrected, and was further supplemented by the French copy of *Das Kapital,* published in Paris, 1873. A French copy was also found in which Marx had indicated the passages he intended to use for the revision of the first volume. This bequest Engels considered as a serious obligation to his lifelong friend.

There were certain problems in the manuscript, which tended to make this a heavy task for Engels. For one thing, the style varied, making it difficult to find a consistent style for the whole book. Some passages were neglected, some illegible; statements were sometimes barely suggested and gaps existed in many places. Several of the subparagraphs had been revised by Marx himself, and, therefore, in addition to the oral instruction he had given to Engels, had to serve as markers showing how far he, Engels, could proceed. By and large, however, Engels concluded, he had been able to stay close to the original work of Marx. Further, Engels asserted that he had not changed a word in the third edition unless he was convinced that Marx would have changed it himself.[363] As he said in the preface to the fourth edition, he had added only a few postscripts to the German text after again comparing the French edition with it, as well as with Marx's handwritten notes. The postscripts were clearly listed. In cases of changes in the historical facts, he had made a few additional glossaries. Other small amendments were only of purely technical nature."[364]

If, however, one reads between the lines of Engels' comments on his contribution to Marx's *Das Kapital,* one is impressed by the enormousness of the work which Engels performed and for which he claimed entirely too little credit. Engels repeatedly remarked that he encountered "small imprecisions" and negligences, discrepancies between the French, English and German texts, Marx's linguistic limitations—although Marx was a linguist—and errors in printing, punctuation and the like.[365]

Of even greater difficulty, more time-and-energy-consuming was Engels' task of putting together the second and third volumes of *Das Kapital.* Here he admitted candidly that he encountered a large number of largely fragmentary treatments. Only one portion (a manuscript marked "IV"), was in a sufficiently finished condition to be put into print. The bulk of the material had been worked out factually, but not gramatically. Much was phrased in the rough which Marx used to prepare outlines, full of colloquialism, and coarse humorous expressions and modes of speech. Side by side with a few very detailed, comprehensive sections were others which were only slightly touched upon. Illustrated material was collected but not classified or integrated into the text; there were incoherent sentences at the ends of chapters and sometimes entire illegible passages, although Engels was quite familiar with his friend's handwriting.[366]

Nonetheless, Engels asserted, he had tried to render Marx's manuscript as literally as possible, to change his style only to the degree that Marx would have approved, and to insert sentences and interlocking statements only where they were absolutely necessary and when the meaning was unmistakable. Modestly Engels stated that all his changes and insertions had hardly amounted to more than ten printed pages and were only of a formal nature.[367] From the photostat manuscript of Engels' "Supplement to *Capital,* Volume III," in the Marx-Engels-Lenin Institute, Moscow, we quote as follows:

> The third volume of *Capital* is receiving many and various interpretations ever since it has been subject to public judgment. It was not to have been expected otherwise. In publishing it, what I was chiefly concerned with was to produce as authentic a text as possible, to exhibit the new

results obtained by Marx in Marx's own words as far as possible, to intervene myself only where absolutely unavoidable, and even then to leave the reader in no doubt as to who was talking to him. This has been criticized. It has been said that I should have converted the material left to me into a systematically written book . . . But this was not how I had conceived my task. I lacked all justification for such a revision; a man like Marx has the right to be heard himself, to transmit his scientific discoveries to posterity in the full genuineness of his own phrasing. Moreover I lacked all desire to infringe—as I had to look upon it—upon the posthumous papers of so pre-eminent a man in such a way: It would have seemed to me a breach of faith. And third, it would have been quite useless.[368]

It is most likely correct when Lenin characterized Engels' great and complicated work for the edition and publication of the second and third volumes of *Das Kapital* as of the two: Marx and Engels."[369]

In spite of the obvious effort on his own part regarding *Das Kapital* Engels was full of praise for it:

As long as there have been capitalists and workers on earth, no book has appeared which is of as much importance for the workers as the one before us. The relation between capital and labor, the hinge on which our entire present system of society turns, is here treated scientifically for the first time, and with a thoroughness and acuity possible only for a German . . . It was reserved for a German to climb to the height from which the whole field of modern social relations can be seen clearly and in full view just as the lower mountain scenery is seen by an observer standing on the topmost peak.[370]

CHAPTER VIII

EPILOGUE: ENGELS VERSUS ENGELS

It has been a relatively uncomplicated task to gather and interpret the raw material of Engels' political thought. Much more complex is the problem before us now: That of reaching a clear and valid conclusion as to how his total accomplishment should be evaluated and recorded in the annals of political theory. The usual tendency has been to lose sight of Engels' significance and independent contribution to the development of socialism, partly because of the degree to which Engels, himself, constantly submerged his own reputation by pointing to the achievements of Marx, almost to the point of self-denial.[371]

To accept such a conclusion, however, taking Engels at his own word, as it were, would be an erroneous underestimation of the man. Those few scholars who, like the Austrian Max Adler, have undertaken to study Engels intensively and with a view to searching out his unique contributions, have come to the conclusion, as we do also, that Engels' importance does not depend solely, and perhaps not even primarily, on his role as interpreter and popularizer of the sometimes difficult and complex ideas of Marx.[372]

However, before we attempt to render our final judgment on this matter of *real* contributions to political thought, a few preliminary comments may be enlightening here to explain why it has come about that, in the popular conception, Engels has been regarded not much more than an *alter ego* of Marx.

As we have already suggested, this misconception was caused largely by Engels himself, through his almost obsequious, overly selfless attitude toward Marx, whom he repeatedly praised as the exclusive author of theoretical socialism.[373] Several times, and in print, Engels emphasized that it was Marx who originated, fully grasped and formulated the materialist conception of history. Thus he wrote in his preface to "The German Peasants War," (published first in the form of articles to the *Neuen Rheinische Zeitung. Politisch-oekonomische Revue,* 1850, and designed to apply the materialist conception of history to an entire historical epoch): "This, the uniquely materialist conception of history, does not come from me (*geht nicht von mir aus*), but from Marx."[374] Similarly Engels alleged in his preface to the English edition of the "Communist Manifesto" of 1888, "the fundamental proposition which forms its nucleus, belongs to Marx."[375]

Engels' voluntary subordination to Marx can be gathered from a number of other statements in which he rated himself modestly below Marx, as, for instance, when he wrote in his preface to "On the Problem of Housing," polemicizing against Proudhon, that Marx would have handled all this much better and more strikingly.[376]

Characteristically, he wrote to Johann Philipp Becker, a personal friend of both men:

I did in my entire life all that which I was destined to do, namely to play the second violin, and I believe that I carried out my assignment quite passably. And I was glad that I had such a splendid violin in Marx . . . None of us has the sharp perception with which he, in the right moment, when quick action was needed, hit the right, and moved toward the decisive target . . . In revolutionary moments his judgment was always incontestable.[377]

When Engels was showered with letters of congratulations in honor of his seventieth birthday, he wrote to the editors of the *Berliner Volksblatt* on December 2, 1890, that it was his destiny to reap the glory and honor for the seeds of which a greater than he, Karl Marx, was responsible.[378]

However, it is our thesis that Engels did not merely play a quietly submissive second fiddle to Marx, but that he did indeed warrant recognition in his own right. On at least one occasion, in a letter to Franz Mehring written from London on July 14, 1893, we find Engels beginning to acknowledge openly that perhaps his own contributions had been minimized while Marx was alive, and seeming to imply that what he was reaping at Marx's death, were bouquets intended for Marx, and not for himself personally. His own proper evaluation he was leaving to history:

. . . (As for) the appendix on historical materialism, in which you have lined up the main things excellently, . . . if I find anything to object to, it is that you give me more credit than I deserve, even if I count everything which I might possibly have found out for myself in time—but which Marx with his more rapid *coup d' oeil* and wider vision discovered much more quickly. When one has the good fortune to work for forty years with a man like Marx, one usually does not *during his lifetime* (underscoring ours) get the recognition one thinks one deserves. Then, when the greater man dies, the lesser easily gets overrated, and this seems to me just my case at present. History will set all this right in the end.[379]

If Engels' *true achievements* were indeed minimized during his lifetime, and he should be credited with being more than merely an interpreter and popularizer of Marx's ideas, on what grounds then should Engels' reputation as a political theorist rest? We believe there are four salient points which can be made about the particular contributions of Engels. And these points are entirely separate from the very important, though human, matter of financial support which, as we know from the correspondence between the two men, Engels so often and generously provided for Marx in order that he might accomplish his work.[380]

1. The first point concerns the matter of political theory, and, in the course of this book, we have shown how Engels arrived at his theory of communism largely independently of Marx. As we stated earlier, Engels reasoned that the Germans arrived at communism by way of philosophy.[381] There is no doubt that Engels identified himself with his fellow-Germans in that respect. As he stated himself in his preface to "The Position," "German socialism and communism more than any other have proceeded from theoretical suppositions; we German theorists still knew too little of the real world to be driven immed-

iately by the real conditions to reforming this 'bad reality'."[382]

One of the purposes of this study, then, has been to show evidence of Engels' contributions to socialist theory by way of philosophy before the period of co-operation with Marx had commenced.[383]

2. A second area of distinct achievement lies in a series of articles now known to have been written by Engels alone. Even after Engels had met Marx, he sometimes undertook to write articles on his own which he sent on to Marx, particularly when Marx explicitly requested them. For instance, when Marx was invited by the American paper, the New York *Daily Tribune,* in August of 1851, to contribute articles, he wrote to Engels, "You must help me now because I have my hands full with the 'Economy'! Write a series of articles on Germany from 1848."[384] Engels accepted and regularly supplied the New York paper with one article after the other. This was the origin of the series "Revolution and Counterrevolution in Germany."[385] E. A. Stepanowa is correct when she stated that only after the publication of the correspondence was it discovered that it was largely Engels, not Marx, who was the author.[386]

3. In addition to assisting Marx occasionally with English translations before the latter acquired a better command of the English language—Marx did not begin to write directly in English before 1853—Engels developed special interests in such matters as military problems, recognizing the significance of military science for future revolutions. In this area, he supplemented Marx, while the latter specialized in problems of foreign affairs. Engels' interest in and knowledge of military science, particularly, became so extensive that this also must be listed among his original contributions preparing the way for the proletarian revolution. In other significant matters, as well, Engels was asked to furnish Marx with information on problems of history, literature and linguistics.[387]

4. A fourth point to be stressed is the fact that Engels contributed far more to the development of socialist theory than merely by supplementing or implementing the work of Marx. Lenin was probably correct, as we have stated earlier, that the second and third volumes of *Das Kapital* were the work of

two persons, Marx and Engels.[388] To prepare the third volume for publication alone took Engels almost ten years. The study of *Das Kapital* reveals that Engels had to make significant additions to Marx's manuscript where the latter had given only sketchy outlines, or where several versions existed for the same topic, although he insisted that he performed this work "exclusively in the spirit of the author." [389] Then there were new editions to be prepared, translated, and prefaced, which involved substantial and original work. Particularly during the twelve years that Engels survived Marx, Engels produced many articles and books of theoretical significance. Thus he published the "Origin of the Family, of Private Property and the State," which was based on data which Marx had collected but had not been able to put together.[390]

Another socialist theoretician, Karl Kautsky, has asserted that he was glad that Engels had written him also on questions of theory which substantially enlarged his knowledge in the most varied fields. Kautsky, generally regarded the most important successor to Marx and Engels, regretted that he was unable to record Engels' words during their conversations, but "these statements still continue to live on in the effects which they exercised upon me."[391] Marx himself in his preface to the French edition (1880) of Engels' "The Revolution of Science" referred to Engels as "one of the most distinguished (*hervorragendst*) representatives of modern socialism."[392]

We hope we have succeeded in making it clear in this study that in more than one sense Engels has contributed significantly to political theory with his ideas on the social revolution, the proletarian state, statelessness, the applicability of scientific dialectics in socio-economic matters, and on materialism.

This study also supports the conclusion that it was in the cooperation between Marx and Engels that Engels' perhaps greatest value rested, qualitatively as well as quantitatively. If we may borrow from Engels' analogy, his significance did not so much consist in his playing purely a violin solo of his own, nor in his playing merely second fiddle some or most of the time, but rather in the continuous co-operation and division of work in the form of a duet between Marx and Engels. As Kautsky wrote on this subject:

Many of their works are the results of joint action. Only a few are exclusively written without any assistance (*Mithilfe*) or influence by the other. The totality of both their literary products formed an intellectual unity. After Marx's death in 1883, his literary legacy devolved upon Engels and thereby the still unpublished sum of works of both friends became a solid unit also externally.[393]

In reviewing the material that has been considered earlier in the book on this question of joint co-operation, let us cite again Engels' assertion, which seems to us accurate, that the "Communist Manifesto" was "our co-operative work."[394] He also wrote that Marx, in his preface to the "Critique of the Political Economy," had described how both of them decided in 1845 to "co-operate" (*gemeinschaftlich ausarbeiten*) on a counter-argument to German ideological philosophy,[395] and how their ensuing joint product, i.e., the "German Ideology," had served its main purpose, namely that of "mutual understanding" (*Selbstverstaendigung*).[396] We have also described, in regard to the materialist conception of history, Engels' report of how both of them in Paris in 1844 had discovered that they had reached the same conclusion, although not through the same channel of reasoning, and that their "co-operative" work dated from that time; they had found out at that time also that they were in "complete agreement" (*vollstaendige Uebereinstimmung*) on all theoretical fields.[397]

Their first jointly written work, in 1845, was "The Holy Family or Critique of Critical Critique. Against Bruno Bauer and Complices" (*Die heilige Familie oder Kritik der Kritischen Kritik. Gegen Bruno Bauer und Konsorten*).[398] Here they criticized the Young Hegelians (Bruno Bauer and Max Stirner) and Hegel's philosophy and idealist philosophy in general. This work marked their final transition from idealism to materialism. When Engels saw Marx ten days later in Paris in 1844, they agreed on the distribution of the chapters to which each wanted to contribute.[399]

95

Kautsky is correct when he reached the conclusion that the co-operation between Marx and Engels which reached its climatic productivity somewhere between August-September 1869 to 1870, especially after Engels had moved to London, cannot be categorized into pedantically distinct compartments of work.[400] Their co-operation took a variety of forms, ranging from formal to informal, as we have repeatedly mentioned in this study. Therefore a blunt distinction between a systematic and scientific Marx versus a more polemical Engels can hardly be sustained. Perhaps recourse should be taken to what Engels himself had to say on this relationship to Marx in his preface to the "Anti-Duehring:"

It was understood between us that *this exposition of mine should not be issued without his knowledge*. I read the whole manuscript to him before it was printed, and the tenth chapter of the part on economics . . . was written by Marx . . . As a matter of fact, *we had always been accustomed to help each other out in special subjects.*[401]

This study has not been aimed at proving or disproving the generally accepted thesis of Marx's pre-eminence and prime significance for the development of scientific socialism. Nor have we found anything intrinsically wrong in Kautsky's allegation that it was the proper division of work between Marx and Engels which enabled the former to concentrate on his *Das Kapital* and other masterpieces.[402] However, we have not found any justification for reducing Engels to not much more than an accessory to Marx. Without detracting from the acknowledged importance of Marx, we have yet demonstrated that a wealth of valuable writings by Friedrich Engels does in fact exist, and while they may be smaller in scope, perhaps less comprehensive, less penetrating, less systematic, less concentrated than the work of Marx, we do maintain that they are sufficiently analytical, and sufficiently original, sufficiently significant, and sufficiently far-reaching in general application and in their lasting effects to entitle Engels to be recognized in his own right. When we consider his independent theoretical grasp of communism, his independent authorship, his implementation of and supplementation to Marx's thoughts, his major original contributions to political theory, and above all, the mutually beneficial co-operation between Marx and himself, Engels rates a far more distinguished place among the founders of the political theory of socialism than previous literature has accorded him.

NOTES

GENERAL INTRODUCTION

1. Cf. Engels' (under the pseudonym "Friedrich Oswald") "Alexander Jung, Vorlesungen ueber die der Deutschen," in *Deutsche Jahrbuecher fuer Wissenschaft und Kunst,* June 15, 1842, cited in Karl Marx and Friedrich Engels, Werke (35 volumes), Institut fuer Marxismus-Leninismus beim ZK der SED; Berlin: Dietz Verlag, 1961 Vol. I, pp. 437-438. (We shall refer to this source from now on as KM/FE — Werke.) For Engels' expressions of solidarity with the Young German Movement, see his letters to Friedrich Graeber, April 28, 1839. Friedrich Engels, *Zwischen 18 und 25; Jugendbriefe von Friedrich Engels,* pp. 73 ff.
2. KM/FE-*Werke,* Vol. II, p 512.
3. *Propylaen-Weltgeschichte,* ed. Walter Goetz, Vol. VII, "Die Franzoesische Revolution, Napoleon, und die Restauration 1789-1848," Propylaen-Verlag, Berlin, 1929, p. 316.

BIOGRAPHICAL INTRODUCTION AND MAIN TEXT

1. Friedrich Engels, "Briefe aus dem Wuppertal," KM/FE-*Werke,* Vol. I, p. 418.
2. Marx-Engels-Lenin-Stalin, *Zur deutschen Geschichte,* Vol. II, 2 HBd., (Berlin: Dietz Verlag, 1954), p. 968. Concerning Engels' objections to pietism and religious orthodoxy, cf. also Friedrich Engels, *Zwischen 18 und 25: Jugendbriefe von Friedrich Engels,* letter from Engels to Friedrich Graeber of April 9, 1839 (p. 76), to Wilhelm Graeber of April 29, 1839 (p. 88), and to Friedrich Graeber of June 15, 1839 (pp. 102, 103 and 105).
3. Vol. I, (2nd rev. ed., Hague, 1934), pp. 9-10.
4. KM/FE-*Werke,* Vol. I, pp. 499-254.
5. KM/FE-*Werke,* Vol. II, pp. 229-506.
6. KM/FE-*Werke,* Vol. XIX, p. 181, f.
7. V. I. Lenin, *Marx-Engels-Marxismus* (Berlin, 1957), pp. 54-55.
8. Friedrich Engels, "Zur Kritik des sozialdemokratischen Programmentwurfes 1891," *Karl Marx: Kritik des Gothaer Programms,* (Berlin: Dietz Verlag, 1955), p. 82.
9. KM/FE-*Werke,* Vol. XXII, pp. 509-527. Cf. Annotation footnote 433, pp. 644-645.
10. "The New Moral World," KM/FE-Werke, I (November 18, 1843), pp. 494-495.
11. "Ein Fragment Fouriers ueber den Handel," KM/FE-*Werke,* II (written between April and the middle of July 1845), p. 607.
12. "Marx und Engels, Deutsche Ideologie, I: Feuerbach," KM/FE-*Werke,* III (written in the spring, 1845), p. 40.
13. *Das Volk,* KM/FE-*Werke,* XIII (August 6, 1859), p. 470 f.
14. "Nachtrag ueber Proudhon und die Wohnungsfrage," KM/FE-*Werke,* XVIII, p. 273.

15. *Ibid.*, p. 277.
16. *Ibid.*, p. 286.
17. *Ibid.*, p. 287.
18. "Einleitung zur englischen Ausgabe (1892): "Die Entwicklung des Sozialismus von der Utopie zur Wissenschaft," KM/FE-*Werke*, XXII, p. 524.
19. "Ergaenzung der Vorbemerkung von 1970 zu 'Der deutsche Bauernkrieg'," KM/FE-*Werke*, XVIII, p. 516.
20. *Ibid.*, p. 517. Cf. Also E. A. Stepanowa, *Friedrich Engels*: *Sein Leben und Werk*, (Berlin: Dietz Verlag, 1958), p. 25.
21. KM/FE-*Werke*, XIX, p. 189.
22. "Die Lage Engels. Thomas Carlyles 'Past and Present'," KM/FE-*Werke*, I, p. 538.
23. *Karl Marx and Frederick Engels, Selected Correspondence*, 1846-1895, The Marxist-Leninist Library 9 (London, 1934), pp. 510-512.
24 *Ibid.*, p. 511.
25. KM/FE-*Werke*, XIV, p. 202.
26. *Ibid.*, p. 202.
27. *Ibid.*, p. 203.
28. *Ibid.*, p. 205.
29. From *Das Volk* (Nr. 16, August 20, 1859), KM/FE-*Werke*, XIII, p. 473 f.
30. KM/FE-*Werke*, XIV, p. 206. Also cf. Gustav Mayer, *Eine Biographie*, Vol. II, p. 309.
31. Gustav Mayer, ibid., p. 310.
32. Friedrich Engels, "Karl Marx: Zur Kritik der Politischen Oekonomie," (*Rezension*), *Das Volk* (Nr. 16, August 20, 1859), KM/FE-*Werke*, XIII, pp. 473-474.
33. *Ibid.*, p. 474. Cf Gustave Mayer, *Eine Biographie*, Vol. II, p. 310.
34. KM/FE-*Werke*, XIII, p. 475.
35. KM/FE-*Werke*, XX, p. 10.
36. *Ibid.*, p. 11
37. KM/FE-*Werke* Vol. XXI, pp. 265-277.
38. *Ibid.*, p. 268.
39. *Ibid.*, p. 270.
40. *Ibid.*, pp. 277-278.
41. *Ibid.*, p. 278.
42. *Ibid.*, p. 279.
43. *Ibid.*, pp. 280-281.
44. *Ibid.*, p. 283.
45. *Ibid.*, p. 285.
46. *Ibid.*, p. 286.
47. *Ibid.*, p. 289.
48. *Ibid.*, p. 290.
49. *Ibid.*, p. 291. See also asterisk on that page.
50. *Ibid.*, p. 292.
51. From *Das Volk* (Nr. 16, August 20, 1859), KM/FE-*Werke*, Vol. XIII, p. 207.
52. Cf. Gustav Mayer, *op. cit.*, Vol. II, p. 322.
53. KM/FE-*Werke*, Vol. 21, p. 263.
54, *Ibid.*, p. 264.
55 KM/FE-*Werke*, Vol. III, pp. 533-535.
56. *Ibid.*, fnte. 1, p. 547.
57. KM/FE-*Werke*, Vol. 21, p. 264.
58. Cf. Gustav Mayer, *op. cit.*, Vol. II, p. 318.

59. *Selected Correspondence,* 1846-1895, *op. cit.,* p. 126.
60. K. Vorlaender, *Karl Marx,* 1929, p. 175 f. Cf. also E. A. Stepanowa, *Friedrich Engels: Sein Leben und Werk,* p. 130.
61. KM/FE-*Werke,* XIX, p. 205.
62. Gustav Mayer, *Eine Biographie,* Vol. II, pp. 319-320. Cf. *Ibid.,* note to p. 319, p. 553.
63. Max Adler, *Engels als Denker,* 2nd rev. ed., (Berlin: Dietz Verlag, 1925), p. 79.
64. Friedrich Engels, *Anti-Duehring: Herr Eugen Duehring's Revolution in Science,* 2nd ed., (Moscow: Foreign Languages Publishing House, 1959), pp. 35-37, Cf. also Max Adler, *op. cit.,* p. 81.
65. KM/FE-*Werke,* XX, p. 11.
66. Karl Marx and Friedrich Engels, *Anti-Duehring, op. cit.,* p. 37.
67. Karl Marx and Friedrich Engels, *Briefwechsel,* Vol. IV, *1868-1883,* (Berlin: Dietz Verlag, 1949), pp. 476-477.
68. Karl Marx/Friedrich Engels, *Anti-Duehring, op. cit.,* p. 19.
69. KM/FE-*Werke,* Vol. XXI, p. 295.
70. *Ibid.,* p. 482.
71. *Ibid.,* pp. 307 (309), 476.
72. *Ibid.,* p. 349.
73. *Ibid.,* p. 514.
74. KM/FE-*Werke,* Vol. XX, pp. 11-12. Cf. also *Anti-Duehring,* pp.17-19.
75. KM/FE-*Werke,* Vol. XX, pp. 10-11.
76. Max Adler, *op. cit.,* p. 25.
77. Friedrich Engels, *Fruehschriften,* p. 188, cited in Max Adler, *op. cit.,* p. 27.
78. *Ibid.,* p. 31.
79. Also in the case of dialectics, Engels did not fail to give its author, Hegel, his due credit. As Engels wrote to Friedrich Langer, a German scientist and political writer, on March 29, 1865, "The modern scientific doctrine of the correlation of natural forces . . . is after all only another expression, or rather it is the positive proof, of the Hegelian development of causes, effects, interaction, force, etc. I am of course no longer a Hegelian, but I still have a great feeling of piety and devotion towards the colossal old chap."
80. KM/FE-*Werke,* Vol. I, pp. 203-333.
81. Cf. Friedrich Engels, "Karl Marx," *Demokratisches Wochenblatt,* Nr. 34, August 21, 1869. Karl Marx and Friedrich Engels, *Ausgewaehlte Schriften,* Vol. I, Berlin: Dietz Verlag, 1955, p. 337.
82. *Ibid.,* pp. 378-391.
83. *Ibid.,* pp. 384-385, 391.
84. KM/FE-*Werke,* VIII, p. 582.
85. *Ibid.,* p. 582.
86. *Ibid.,* p. 583.
87. *Ibid.,* p. 584. Also Max Adler, *Engels als Denker,* p. 88. Adler rejects Engels' allegation that Marx deserves most of the credit for the theory of materialism. In reference to the theory of materialism cf. also Franz Mehring, *Karl Marx, Geschichte seines Lebens,* Leipzig, 1918, pp. 99: ". . . in their prime, Engels did the giving and Marx the receiving in a field in which ultimately the decisive battle had to be waged."
88. KM/FE-*Werke,* VIII, p. 584.
89. Marx-Engels, *Ausgewaehlte Schriften in zwei Baenden,* Vol. II, (Berlin, 1958), p. 320.
90. Karl Marx, *Zur Kritik der politischen Oekonomie,* (Berlin: Dietz Verlag, 1951), p. 14.

91. Max Adler, *op. cit.*, pp. 35-37.
92. e.g., cf. Horst Ullrich, *Der Junge Engels: Eine historisch bio-graphische Studie seiner weltanschaulichen Entwicklung in den Jahren 1834-1845*, Berlin: VEB Deutscher Verlag der Wissenschaften, 1966, Vol. II, pp. 32-33.
93. Karl Marx/Friedrich Engels: *Historisch-Kritische Gesamtausgabe* (MEGA), I, Part 2, (Berlin, 1930), p. 223.
94. KM/FE-*Werke*, III, pp. 17, 19, 20.
95. *Ibid.*, p. 20.
96. *Ibid.*, p. 38.
97. *Ibid.*, p. 40, 41.
98. *Ibid.*, p. 49, 50.
99. *Ibid.*, pp. 113-114.
100. KM/FE-*Werke*, XIII, pp. 473-474.
101. KM/FE-*Werke*, III, pp. 20-21.
102. *Ibid.*, p. 21.
103. *Ibid.*, pp. 21-24.
104. *Ibid.*, p. 25.
105. *Ibid.*, p. 26.
106. *Ibid.*, p. 26.
107. *Ibid.*, p. 27. Also cf. pp. 30-32.
108. *Ibid.*, p. 37.
109. *Ibid.*, p. 38, 40.
110. *Ibid.*, pp. 42-43, 46.
111. *Selected Correspondence, op. cit.*, pp. 516 ff.
112. KM/FE-*Werke*, XIX, p. 210.
113. Marx/Engels, *Ausgewaehlte Briefe*, (Berlin, 1953), p. 502.
114. Cf. also Engels' letter to Conrad Schmidt, a German social democrat, one of the founders of the journal *Sozialistische Monatshefte*, October, 27, 1890.
115. Friedrich Engels, "Karl Marx: Zur Kritik der politischen Oekonomie," (Rezension), XIII, 471.
116. *Selected Correspondence, op. cit.*, p. 473.
117. KM/FE-*Werke*, VII, pp. 511-512.
118. *Ibid.*, p. 512.
119. "Die Rolle der Gewalt in der Geschichte," written by Engels at the end of December 1887 until March 1888. KM/FE-*Werke*, XXI, p. 410 f.
120. Cf. Engels' letter to Conrad Schmidt, October 27, 1890, in which Engels discusses the impact of economics on political power and law, in *Selected Correspondence, op., cit.*, pp. 480-481.
121. KM/FE-*Werke*, XXII, p. 292.
122. *Ibid.*, p. 298.
123. Friedrich Engels, "Grundsaetze des Kommunismus," KM/FE-*Werke*, IV, p. 372.
124. "Die Lage Englands," KM/FE-*Werke*, I, p. 531.
125. "Stellung der politischen Partei," *Ibid.*, p. 461.
126. "Die inneren Krisen," *Ibid.*, p. 460.
127. Marx and Engels, *Ausgewaehlte Briefe*, (Berlin, 1953), p. 540.
128. *Selected Correspondence, op. cit.*, pp. 505-506.
129. "Der Status Quo in Deutschland," KM/FE-*Werke*, IV, pp. 40-47.
130. *Ibid.*, pp. 378-379.
131. "Zur Wohnungsfrage," Zweiter Abschmitt, KM/FE-*Werke*, XVIII, pp. 238 ff, 248-249.
132. "Die Entwicklung des Sozialismus," KM/FE-*Werke*, XIX, pp. 194-195.

133. *Ibid.*, p. 196.
134. *Ibid.*, p. 197 f. Cf. also "Zwei Reden in Elberfeld," *Ibid.*, II, pp. 545-546.
135. "Anti-Duehring," KM/FE-*Werke*, XX, pp. 272 ff.
136. "Zur Wohnungsfrage," Dritter Abschnitt, KM/FE-*Werke*, XVIII, p. 282.
137. "Die Entwicklung," etc. KM/FE-*Werke*, XXX, p. 191.
138. "Lage der arbeitenden Klasse in England," KM/FE-*Werke*, II, p. 452. Cf. also Friedrich Engels, *Briefe an Bebel*. (Berlin: Institut fuer Marxismus-Leninismus beim ZK der SED, Dietz Verlag, 1958), Engels' letter to August Bebel, Wilhelm Liebknecht, Wilhelm Bracke and others, from London, September 17/18, 1879. Engels defended the idea of a "one-sided" proletarian revolution and polemicized against erudites and humanitarians (pp. 34-35). Engels stressed the ability of the working class to liberate and lead itself without outside help from the upper echelon of society. *Ibid.*, p. 36.
139. KM/FE-*Werke*, XIX, pp. 200-201.
140. *Anti-Duehring*, p. 351.
141. *Ibid.*, p. 352.
142. *Ibid.*, p. 534.
143. *Ibid.*, p. 365.
144. *Selected Correspondence, op. cit.*, pp. 113-114. Cf.
145. "Die Entwicklung," etc., KM/FE-*Werke*, XIX, p. 208.
146. *Ibid.*, p. 208.
147. KM/FE-*Werke*, II, pp. 521 ff.
148. "Die Lage der arbeitenden Klasse," etc., *Ibid.*, p. 430.
149. "Das kuerzliche Gemetzel in Leipzig," *Ibid.*, p. 560.
150. "Deutsche Zustaende," KM/FE-*Werke*, III, p. 580.
151. "Deutsche Ideologie: I, Feuerbach," *Ibid.*, p. 32.
152. *Ibid.*, p. 33.
153. *Ibid.*, p. 34.
154. *Ibid.*, p. 74.
155. KM/FE-*Werke*, XIX, pp. 207-208.
156. "Zur Wohnungsfrage," etc., KM/FE-*Werke*, XVIII, p. 268.
157. "Die preussische Militaerfrage und die deutsche Arbeiterpartei," KM/FE-*Werke*, XVI, p. 76.
158. "Die Bewegungen von 1847," KM/FE-*Werke*, IV, pp. 502-503.
159. "Schutzzoll oder Freihandels-System," *Ibid.*, pp. 60-61. The notion of democracy as an intermediary stage was also expressed in Engels' "Der Kommunisten-Prozess zu Koeln," KM/FE-*Werke*, VIII, p. 399.
160. KM/FE-*Werke*, IV, p. 61. Cf. also E. A. Stepanowa, *op. cit.*, p. 55.
161. "Anti-Duehring." "Zweiter Abschnitt: Politische Oekonomie," KM/FE-*Werke*, XX, p. 152.
162. "Deutsche Ideologie," KM/FE-*Werke*, III, p. 46.
163. *Ibid.*, p. 46 f.
164. *Ibid.*, p. 69 f. This is comparable to one of Marx's earliest statements concerning classes and the class war which preceded the *Communist Manifesto* by a year. It is contained in his "Misère de la Philosophie," published in the summer of 1847. (KM/FE-*Werke*, Vol. IV, pp. 181-182). Marx explained how modern economic conditions were responsible for the creation of class antagonism between capital and labor, similarly as the bourgeoisie came into existence as a result of a clash between feudalism and absolute monarchism. Every economic class in history, Marx asserted, was compelled to overthrow the old society in order to gain political power. The proletariat, which must abolish the bourgeoisie in the course of economic development, however, would end the re-occurrence of clashes

of antagonistic classes, by replacing *all* classes by an association in which all class contrasts would end. Until this process had come about, however, The clash between proletariat and bourgeoisie a battle of class against class, a battle which in its extreme form will mean a total revolution. . . . Only when there are no classes and class conflicts will the societal evolutions cease to be political revolutions. (*Ibid.*, p. 182.).

165. *Ibid.*, p. 189.
166. Cf. also "Anti-Duehring." "Dritter Abschnitt: Sozialismus," KM/FE-*Werke*, XX, p. 239 f., in which Engels challenged rationalism of the French Revolution: "This eternal rationalism in reality was nothing but the idealized brain of the middle class man, developing at that time toward the bourgeoisie." Engels pointed out the decline of "fraternity" and other principles of the French Revolution. At the turn of the century disappointment about the "victory of rationalism" was clearly stated, such as by Saint-Simon, Fourier and Owen.
167. KM/FE-*Werke*, III, pp. 190-191, 196.
168. *Ibid.*, p. 194.
169. *Anti-Duehring*, pp. 133-147.
170. *Ibid.*, p. 134.
171. *Ibid.*, p. 136.
172. *Ibid.*, p. 138.
173. *Ibid.*, p. 142.
174. *Ibid.*, pp. 142-143.
175. *Ibid.*, p. 147.
176. *Ibid.*, p. 148.
177. *Selected Correspondence, op. cit.*, p. 435.
178. "Fortschritte der Sozialreform auf dem Kontinent," KM/FE-*Werke*, I, p. 481.
179. "Die Lage Englands. Thomas Carlyle's 'Past and Present,' " *Ibid.*, p. 537. Cf. also "Die Lage Englands. Die englische Konstitution," *Ibid.*, p. 574. *Ibid.*, p. 577.
180. *Ibid.*, p. 591. Cf. also "Deutsche Zustaende," KM/FE-*Werke*, II, p. 579, and E. A. Stepanowa, *op. cit.*, p. 29.
181. Eduard Bernstein (ed.), *Die Briefe von Friedrich Engels an Eduard Bernstein, mit Briefen von Karl Kautsky an ebendenselben.* Herausgegeben von Eduard Bernstein. (Berlin: Dietz Verlag. 1925), March 24, 1884, p. 142.
182. "Die Lage Englands. Die englische Konstitution," KM/FE-*Werke*, I, pp. 571 ff.
183. *Ibid.*, pp. 573-574. Cf. also "Die Lage der arbeitenden Klasse in England, Arbeiterbewegungen," KM/FE-*Werke*, I, pp. 571 ff.
183. *Ibid.*, pp. 573-574. Cf. also "Die Lage der arbeitenden Klasse in England, Arbeiterbewegungen," KM/FE-*Werke*, II, p. 445.
184. Friedrich Engels, *Briefe an Bebel, op. cit.*, pp. 36-37.
185. *Ibid.*, p. 37.
186. *Ibid.*, p. 41. Cf. also "zur Wohnungsfrage," KM/FE-*Werke*, XVIII, p. 263.
187. Friedrich Engels, *Briefe an Bebel*, p. 40. Cf. also "Die englische Zehnstundenbill," KM/FE-*Werke*, VII, p. 241.
188. "Die englische Konstitution," KM/FE-*Werke*, I, p. 592. Cf. also "Zwei Reden in Elberfeld," KM/FE-*Werke*, II, p. 555.
189. "Das Fest der Nationen in London," *Ibid.*, p. 613.
190. "Zwei Reden in Elberfeld," *Ibid.*, pp. 555-556.
191. KM/FE-*Werke*, Vol. I, p. 388.
192. *Ibid.*, p. 389.
193. *Ibid.*, p. 390.

194. *Ibid.*, p. 394.
This may be compared with Marx's "Kritik des Gothaer Programms," (Criticism of the Gotha Program), written in 1875, which include his thoughts on the socialist revolution, the dictatorship of the proletariat and the transition from capitalism to communism. One of his major theses is the historical inevitability of a transitional stage: "Between the capitalist and communist society lies a period of revolutionary change of one into the other. To this corresponds also a political transitional period in which the state cannot be anything else but the revolutionary dictatorship of the proletariat." (KM/FE-*Werke,* Vol. XIX, p. 28.)

195. "Englische Ansicht ueber die inneren Krisen," KM/FE-*Werke,* I, (December 8, 1842), pp. 454-455.

196. "Die innern Krisen," *Ibid.,* (December 9, 1842), p. 457.

197. "Zur Wohnungsfrage," KM/FE-*Werke,* XVIII, pp. 243 ff.

198. KM/FE-*Werke,* I, (December 10, 1842), p. 460. In the "German Ideology" Marx and Engels distinguished between three related functions of a social revolution: 1. the revolution as a power to destroy the former modes of bourgeois production; 2. the revolution as a dynamic scene in which the energies of the proletariat are developed; 3. the revolution as a process in which the proletariat divorces itself from what adhered to it from its former social position. *Vide* KM/FE-*Werke,* III, p. 68.

199. *Ibid.*, p. 525 ff.

200. *Ibid.*, p. 550.

201. *Vorwort* to "Die Lage Englands, etc.," KM/FE-*Werke,* II, pp. 233-234.

202. *Ibid.*, pp. 237-255.

203. *Ibid.*, pp. 256-305.

204. *Ibid.*, pp. 306-319. Cf. Max Adler, *op. cit.,* p. 44.

205. KM/FE-*Werke,* II, p. 306.

206. *Ibid.*, p. 312.

207. *Ibid.*, *p.* 318.

208. *Ibid.*, pp. 324-359, 465.

209. *Ibid.*, p. 343.

210. *Ibid.*, p. 349.

211. *Ibid.*, p. 372. Cf. also "Die englische Zehnstundenbill," KM/FE-*Werke,* VII, pp. 242-243.

212. "Briefe aus dem Wuppertal," KM/FE-*Werke,* I, pp. 417 ff., published in the *Telegraph fuer Deutschland.*

213. *op. cit.,* p. 6.

214. KM/FE-*Werke,* I, p. 456.

215. KM/FE-*Werke,* II, p. 229. cf. also KM/FE-*Werke,* VIII, p. 590 Friedrich Engels, *Fruehschriften,* pp. 276-277. *Neue Zeit, Jahrgang* 28, KM/FE-*Werke,* I, p. 427. Cf. Max Adler, op. cit., p. 41. Also in "Zwei Reden in Elberfeld," II, pp. 549-550. *Vide* "Deutsche Ideologie," III, pp. 70, 77; "Die Zehnstundenfrage," VII, p. 230 f.

216. *op. cit.,* p. 130.

217. KM/FE-*Werke,* I, Nr. 19, November 4, 1843, pp. 480-481.

218. Correspondence with Bernstein, p. 130. Cf. also KM/FE-*Werke,* Vol. XVIII, pp. 565-566, "Fluechtlingsliteratur: Soziales aus Russland."

219. *Anti-Duehring,* p. 221.

220. *Ibid.*, p. 224.

221. *Ibid.*, p. 226.

222. *Ibid.*, p. 228.

223. *Ibid.*, p. 252.

224. KM/FE-*Werke,* XIX, p. 228.

225. KM/FE-*Werke,* XX, pp. 273 ff.

226. Ibid., 273-277.
227. KM/FE-*Werke*, VII, pp. 516-517.
228. "Einleitungen zu 'Karl Marx: Die Klassenkaempfe in Frankreich' (Ausgabe 1895)" *Ibid.*, p. 523.
229. KM/FE-*Werke*, IV, pp. 374-375. Cf. also E. A. Stepanowa, p. 57.
230. KM/FE-*Werke*, III, p. 35.
231. KM/FE-*Werke*, XVIII, pp. 556-557. This article was published in *Der Volksstaat* Nr. 43, April 16. 1875.
232. *Ibid.*, pp. 560, 556-567.
233. *Ibid.*, p. 668.
234. *Selected Correspondence, op. cit.*, p. 437.
235. *Ibid.*, p. 508.
236. Cf. Friedrich Engels, "Vorwort zur 4. deutschen Ausgabe des 'Manifests der Kommunistischen Partei'," (dated January 21, 1882), KM/FE-*Werke*, XXII, p. 55.
237. KM/FE-*Werke*, XVIII, p. 308.
238. "Von der Autoritaet," *Ibid.*, p. 308.
239. KM/FE-*Werke*, XIX, pp. 20, 28.
240. Yet cf. Friedrich Engels, "Die Lage Englands. Die englische Konstitution," KM/FE-*Werke*, I, p. 572 in which he recommended that one look at the *state* as something "inhuman" which ought to be abolished, instead of looking at the *form* of state that only needed to be changed ("humanized").
241. *Neue Zeit*, (Bd. I, 1913-1914), p. 40.
242. Nijegaars Nieuwenhuis, "Der staatssozialistische Charakter der Sozialdemokratie," Archiv fuer *Sozialwissenschaft und-politik*, Vol. XXVIII; Hans Kelsen, *Sozialismus und Staat; eine Untersuchung der politischen Theorie des Marxismus, Sozialismus und Staat*, (2nd ed., Leipzig, 1923) p. 104; cf. also Helmuth Lohmann, *Der Staat bei Friedrich Engels*, Dissertation University of Cologne, 1958, p. 86.
243. *Correspondence with Bernstein, op. cit.*, p. 137.
244. *Selected Correspondence, op. cit.*, p. 321.
245. Written between October 1872 and March 1873, KM/FE-*Werke*, XVIII, pp. 305 ff.
246. *Ibid.*, p. 308.
247. *Ibid.*, pp. 476 ff.
248. *Ibid.*, p. 479.
249. *Ibid.*, pp. 493-494.
250. *Ibid., Selected Correspondence, op. cit.*, p. 319 f. Cf. also Engels' letter to Cuno in Marx/Engels: *Ausgewaehlte Briefe*, (Berlin, 1953), p. 329.
251. *Selected Correspondence*, pp. 416-417, Also in KM/FE-*Werke*, XIX, pp. 344-435. Cf. also XXXIII, pp. 365-366, 374-375, 388-389, 655-657, 668.
252. "Einleitung zu 'Die Klassenkaempfe in Frankreich,' (Ausgabe 1895)," KM/FE-*Werke*, VII, pp. 514 ff.
253. "Der Ursprung der Familie, des Privateigentums und des Staats," KM/FE-*Werke*, XXI, pp. 165-167.
254. *Ibid.*, p. 168.
255. *Ibid.*, pp. 302 ff.
256. *Ibid.*, p. 300. Cf. "Zur Wohnungsfrage. Zweiter Abschnitt," KM/FE-*Werke*, XVIII, p. 258, in which Engels admitted that "to some degree" Germany still was a state in which the bourgeoisie did not rule yet, and where consequently the common interests of the society, rather than of a single class were represented.
257. KM/FE-*Werke*, IV, p. 33.
258. *Ibid.*, p. 62. Cf also p. 69.

259. KM/FE-*Werke*, XVII, pp. 623-625 (Ausgabe 1891). In his introduction (Einleitung) Engels analyzed the historical, theoretical and practical significance of the Parisian Commune. Observe Engels' concluding sentence: "Well, Gentlemen, if you desire to know what a dictatorship looks like, look at the Parisian Commune. This was the dictatorship of the proletariat." Ibid., p. 625. Cf. also annotation on pp. 703-704.

260. "Grundsaetze des Kommunismus," (written October-November, 1847), KM/FE-*Werke*, IV, pp. 372-374. Engels outlined the development of the revolution with the express assumption that the proletariat would operate initially at least within the framework of a democratic constitutional system. One might argue that Engels' suggested gradualness was in conflict with his advertised social revolution.

261. Note that Lenin considered this part of Engels' letter to Bebel "the most remarkable observation in the works of Marx and Engels on the state." In V. I. Lenin, *Ausgewaehlte Werke in zwei Baenden*, Vol. II, Berlin, 1955, p. 206.

262. KM/FE-*Werke*, XIX, p. 7.

263. *Ibid.*, p. 223.

264. *Ibid.*, p. 224.

265. *Ibid.*, p. 223.

266. *Ibid.*, p. 224.

267. *Ibid.*, p. 224.

268. *Ibid.*, pp. 223-224 and *Anti-Duehring, op. cit.*, pp. 386-387.

269. E. A. Stepanowa, *op. cit.*, p. 214.

270. Cf. also KM/FE-*Werke*, XIII, p. 10.

271. KM/FE-*Werke*, III, p. 46.

272. KM/FE-*Werke*, XXI, p. 299; in Engels' "Ludwig Feuerbach und der Ausgang der klassischen deutschen Philosophie" he qualified this relationship between class and changing economic conditions, by admitting that one might at least "at first look" ascribe the rise of feudal landownership to political, not economic, circumstances, i.e., by the seizure of land by act of violence. The clash between feudalism and bourgeoisie, as between bourgeoisie and proletariat, was more clearly conditioned by "purely" economic causes.

273. KM/FE-*Werke*, XIX, p. 208 f. Cf. also "Der Status Quo in Deutschland," KM/FE-*Werke*, IV, p. 50 f.

274. *Briefe an Bebel, op. cit.*, London, March 18/28, 1875; also KM/FE-*Werke*, XIX, p. 7.

275. "Anti-Duehring, Zweiter Abschnitt. Politische Oekonomie," KM/FE-Werke, XX, pp. 137 ff.

276. *Ibid.*, pp. 166 ff.

277. "Der Ursprung der Familie," etc., KM/FE-*Werke*, XXI, p. 68.

278. *Ibid.*, pp. 168 ff.

279. *Ibid.*, pp. 273 ff.

280. *Ibid.*, p. 274.

281. *Ibid.*, pp. 511-512.

282. KM/FE-*Werke*, IV, pp. 375-376.

283. "Zur Wohnungsfrage," KM/FE-*Werke*, XVIII, p. 221.

284. "Zwei Reden in Elberfeld," KM/FE-*Werke*, II, p. 539.

285. Ibid., p. 543.

286. *Ibid.*, p. 544.

287. *Ibid.*, p. 542.

288. "Die preussische Militaerfrage und die deutsche Arbeiterpartei," KM/FE-*Werke*, XVI, p. 69. Also cf. "Anti-Duehring," XX, p. 276.

289. "Deutsche Ideologie," KM/FE-*Werke*, III, pp. 74-75.

290. KM/FE-*Werke*, IV, pp. 370-371.

291. KM/FE-*Werke*, II, p. 545.
292. *Ibid.*, p. 545.
293. *Ibid.*, p. 546.
294. KM/FE-*Werke*, XVIII, p. 22.
295. *Ibid.*, p. 243.
296. *Ibid.*, pp. 263, 226-277. The existing problems of housing, including shortages, slums, excessive rents, etc., were blamed by Engels on the capitalist system. Cf. *Ibid.*, p. 236.
297. "Grundsaetze des Kommunismus," KM/FE-*Werke*, IV, p. 377.
298. KM/FE-*Werke*, XXIII, p. 514.
299. KM/FE-*Werke*, XX, p. 296.
300. E. A. Stepanowa, *op. cit.*, p. 20.
301. *Ibid.*, p. 216.
302. KM/FE-*Werke*, I, pp. 544-546.
303. *Ibid.*, p. 545.
304. *Ibid.*, p. 545.
305. *Ibid.*, p. 546.
306. *Idib.*, p. 546.
307. *Ibid.*, p. 547.
308. "Fortschritte der Sozialreform auf dem Kontinent," KM/FE-*Werke*, I, p. 487.
309. KM/FE-*Werke*, XXII, pp. 292-298.
310. "Fluechtlingsliteratur II, Programm der blanquistischen Kommunistenfluechtlinge," KM/FE-*Werke*, XVIII, pp. 531-532.
311. "Ludwig Feuerbach und der Ausgang der klassischen deutschen Philosophie," KM/FE-*Werke*, XXI, pp. 303, 305.
312. KM/FE-*Werke*, IV, p. 465.
313. "Lage der arbeitenden Klasse in England," KM/FE-*Werke*, II, pp. 352-353.
314. "Bruno Bauer und das Urchristentum," KM/FE-*Werke*, XIX, p. 297.
315. *Ibid.*, p. 298.
316. "Zur Geschichte des Urchristentums," KM/FE-*Werke*, XXII, p. 449 f.
317. Dritter Abschnitt: "Sozialismus V: Staat, Familie, Erziehung," KM/FE-*Werke*, XX, pp. 294-295.
318. *Ibid.*, p. 295.
319. KM/FE-*Werke*, XIX, pp. 210 ff.
320. KM/FE-*Werke*, XXIII, pp. 331-530.
321. KM/FE-*Werke*, XIX, p. 214.
322. KM/FE-*Werke*, XXIII, pp. 459, 486, 511.
323. Ibid., p. 675.
324. KM/FE-*Werke*, XIX, p. 221.
325. *Ibid.*, p. 223. Cf. also XXII, p. 209, "Einleitung zu Marx' 'Lohnarbeit und Kapital.' "
326. "Umrisse zu einer Kritik der Nationaloekonomie," KM/FE-*Werke*, I, pp. 494-524. Observe that Engels asserted that, although the application of the doctrine of surplus value "leads directly to Communism," Marx never founded his communist demands on the doctrine of surplus value but instead on the rapidly collapsing capitalist method of production. The doctrine of surplus value, suggested Engels, belonged more appropriately to a moral application in economics, in the sense that the economic fact of the unpaid surplus value violated the workers' "moral feeling." Cf. IV, p. 561, "Vorwort zu Karl Marx: 'Das Elend der Philosophie.' "
327. *Ibid.*, pp. 510-512.

328. *Ibid.*, pp. 499-524.
329. *Ibid.*, p. 512. Cf. also XXII, p. 208.
330. KM/FE-*Werke*, XIX, p. 209.
331. *Ibid.*, p. 209.
332. *Ibid.*, pp. 247-250. Cf. also XXII, pp. 208-209, "Einleitung, etc.," Cf. also XVIII, p. 214, "Zur Wohnungsfrage."
333. "Vorwort zu Karl Marx: Das Elend, etc.," KM/FE-*Werke*, IV, pp. 560-561.
334. KM/FE-*Werke*, XVIII, p. 214.
335. KM/FE-*Werke*, XIX, p. 209.
336. KM/FE-*Werke*, XXI, p. 3.
337. *Ibid.*, p. 3, also p. 357, IV, p. 581.
338. *Ibid.*, pp. 357-358.
339. *Ibid.*, pp. 3-4, asterisk, Annotation of Engels to the German edition of 1890.
340. *Ibid.*, p. 358. Also IV, p. 582.
341. *Selected Correspondence*, p. 21.
342. *Ibid.*, pp. 20-21.
343. KM/FE-*Werke*, IV, p. 640, footnote 237.
344. Marx/Engels, *Ausgewaehlte Schriften in zwei Baenden*, Vol. II, Berlin, 1958, p. 323.
345. *Selected Correspondence*, p. 20.
346. KM/FE-*Werke*, XXII, p. 58.
347. "Die preussische Militaerfrage," etc., KM/FE-*Werke*, XVI, p. 70. Also "Grundsaetze des Kommunismus," IV, p. 369; *Ibid.*, p. 364 re. the capitalist factory system.
348. "Der internationale Sozialismus und der italienische Sozialismus," KM/FE-*Werke*, XXII, p. 479.
349. "Einleitung zu Marx' 'Klassenkaempfe', " etc., *Ibid.*, p. 513 f.
350. "Grundsaetze," etc., KM/FE-*Werke*, IV, p. 368.
351. "Die Lage der arbeitenden Klassen in England," KM/FE-*Werke*, II, p. 254.
352. *Ibid.*, pp. 306 ff. Also cf. "Zwei Reden in Elberfeld," II, pp. 536.
353. *Ibid.*, p. 572.
354. *Ibid.*, p. 504.
355. *Ibid.*, p. 505. Cf. also p. 550.
356. KM/FE-*Werke*, Vol. XXI, p. 263.
357. *Ibid.*, pp. 291-292.
358. *Ibid.*, p. 328.
359. KM/FE-*Werke*, Vol. XX, p. VIII.
360. 2nd edition, Foreign Languages Publishing House, Moscow, 1959, p. 10.
361. W. I. Lenin, *Werke*, Vol. 2, Berlin, 1961, p. 11.
362. KM/FE-*Werke*, XXIII, pp. 33 f.
363. *Ibid.*, p. 34.
364. *Ibid.*, p. 41.
365. *Ibid.*, p. 42.
366. In a letter to Lavrov Engels complained that he was the only man who could decipher Marx's handwriting and abbreviations of words and sentences. Cf. Marx und Engels, *Brief ueber das Kapital*, (Berlin: Dietz Verlag, 1954), p. 284.
367. KM/FE-*Werke*, XXIV, p. 7.
368. Friedrich Engels, *Supplement to Capital*, Vol. III, 1895, from photostat manuscript, "Ergaenzung und Nachtrag zum III. Band des Kapital," p. 94.
369. V. I. Lenin, Marx-Engels-Marxismus (Berlin, 1957), p. 54.

Note that Marx used Engels' data of the British factory system of 1845 ("The Position of the Working Class in England") for his descriptions and illustrations of British economics in his *Das Kapital*: "I need not dwell much on the period of big industry in England until 1845, and refer the reader to Friedrich Engels' 'The Position of the Working Class in England', Leipzig, 1845. How deeply Engels grasped the spirit of the capitalist mode of production is demonstrated by the Factory Reports, Reports on Mines, etc., which appeared since 1845. How remarkably he depicted the conditions in detail is demonstrated . . . by the official Reports of the Children's Employment Commission which were published eighteen to twenty years later." KM/FE-*Werke*, XXIII, p. 254. Note also Kautsky's statement regarding Engels' "Anti-Duehring," that "only through the 'Anti-Duehring' have we truly learned and understood the *Kapital.*" In *Friedrich Engels' Briefwechsel mit Karl Kautsky, Vienna*: Danubia Verlag, 1955, p. 4.

370. From Engels' article in *Leipziger Demokratisches Wochenblatt*, No. 12, May 21, 1888, in *Engels on Capital: Synopsis, Reviews, Letters and Supplementary Material* (N.Y.: International Publishers, 1937), p. 3. (Translation by L. E. Mins).

371. Max Adler, *op. cit.*, p. 5.

372. *Ibid.*, p. 15.

373. *Ibid.*, p. 15.

374. "Vorbemerkung zu 'Deutsche Bauernkrieg,' Ausgabe 1870 und 1875," KM/FE-*Werke*, VII, p. 532. Compare this with Marx's introduction to his "Kritik der Hegelschen Rechtsphilosophie" in which his views on the nature of religion may be summed up by his own statement that religion was "the opium of the people." Religion which Marx proposed to subject to merciless criticism, was made by man, not that man was made by religion, man being not an abstract being but part of "the world of men, state and society." KM/FE-*Werke*, p. 378. Religion was "the sigh of the oppressed creature, the sentiment of a heartless world, as it is the spirit of spiritless conditions." *Ibid.*, p. 378. Marx asked that religion be recognized as "illusionary," in order to enable man to pursue his "real" happiness, to think and to act like a man to whom was accorded reasoning powers. It was the duty of history, Marx wrote, to establish the truth of the life "on this side." Ibid., p. 379. Religion must be abrogated in order to restore to man his power to apply reason and reality to the solution of his social problems, in order to cease being a "degraded, servile, neglected and contemptible being," and in order to recognize as untenable the concept that "man was the highest essence for men." (*Ibid.*, p. 385).

375. KM/FE-*Werke*, XXI, p. 357.

376. KM/FE-*Werke*, XVIII, p. 650.

377. Friedrich Engels, *Vergessene Briefe*, (Berlin, 1922), p. 55. Also in E. A. Stepanowa, *op. cit.*, p. 219.

378. Max Adler, *op. cit.*, p. 15; Karl Kautsky, *Friedrich Engels, sein Leben, sein Wirken, seine Schriften*, (Berlin: Verlag Buchhandlung Vorwaerts, 1908), p. 27. Cf. Also *Das Berliner Volksblatt*, Nr. 284, December 5, 1890.

379. Selected Correspondence, p. 510. Engels' letter referred to Mehring's article "On Historical Materialism," which was published as an appendix to the first edition of his book, *Die Lessingslegende*.

380. Marx/Engels *Briefwechsel* Vol. III: *1861-1867*, (Berlin, 1950), p. 333. Cf. V. I. Lenin, *Marx-Engels Marxismus*, (Berlin, 1957), pp. 5-45.

381. *Neue Zeit*, Jahrgang 28, 1. Band, 1843, pp. 427-428.

382. KM/FE-*Werke*, II, p. 233. Cf. also Max Adler, *op., cit.*, footnote of p. 50. Cf. also Engels' letter to Karl Marx, January 20, 1849, in

which Engels also wrote about "us theoretical Germans," F. E., *Zwischen 18 und 25, op. cit.,* p. 249.
383. *Ibid.,* p. 16.
384. Marx/Engels *Briefwechsel* Vol. I, *1848-1855,* (Berlin, 1949), p. 295.
385. Marx/Engels/Lenin/Stalin: *Zur deutschen Geschichte,* Vol. II, 1. Adb., (Berlin, 1954), pp. 351-468. Also pp. 108-111.
386. E. A. Stepanowa, *op. cit.,* pp. 119-120. Cf. KM/FE-*Werke,* XXVII, pp. 656-657, footnote 256.
387. E. A. Stepanowa, *op. cit.,* pp. 120-121.
388. V. I. Lenin, *Marx-Engels-Marxismus,* (Berlin, 1957), p. 54. Cf. also E. A. Stepanowa, p. 151, who points out that Marx in writing his *Kapital* asked for Engels' assistance also on the most important *theoretical* problems and reached his conclusions from correspondence with Engels.
389. Karl Marx, *Das Kapital,* Vol. II, (Berlin, 1957), p. 6. Cf. KM/FE-*Werke,* XXIII, pp. 33-34, 41-42.
390. Marx and Engels, *Ausgewaehlte Schriften in zwei Baenden,* Vol. II, (Berlin, 1958), pp. 159-304.
391. Karl Kautsky, *Fruehzeit des Marxismus, Briefwechsel Engels-Kautsky,* herausgegeben und erlaeutert von K. Kautsky, (Prague: Orbin Verlag, A.G., 1935), p. 400.
392. KM/FE-*Werke,* XIX, p. 181.
393. Karl Kautsky, *op. cit.,* p. 395. Lenin may be cited here, too, who in his "The Marx-Engels Correspondence: Engels as one of the Founders of Communism," wrote in October 1913 that their correspondence (1844-1883) was of "tremendous" scientific and political value. Lenin ascribed much of this value to their discussions and debates on the most important principles of the political tasks of the working class. In V.I. Lenin, *Selected Works,* Vol. II, pp. 42 ff.
394. KM/FE-*Werke,* XXI, p. 357.
395. *Ibid.,* p. 263.
396. *Ibid.,* p. 263; cf. also XIII, p. 10.
397. Marx and Engels, *Ausgewaehlte Schriften,* etc., Vol. II, (Berlin: Dietz Verlag, 1958), pp. 319-320.
398. KM/FE-*Werke,* II, pp. 3-323.
399. Cf. table of contents to KM/FE-*Werke,* II, pp. 723-725, from which the authorship for each chapter can be gleaned. It is of no consequence for our study to observe that Marx contributed more than Engels to the *Heilige Familie.*
400. Karl Kautsky, *Friedrich Engels, sein Leben,* etc., p. 26.
401. Karl Kautsky, *op. cit.,* p. 14. Underscoring added; cited also in K. Kautsky, *op. cit.,* p. 26.
402. *Ibid.,* p. 27.

BIBLIOGRAPHY

Adler, Georg: *Geschichte des Sozialismus und Kommunismus*, Leipzig, 1899.
Adler, Max: *Staatsauffassung des Marxismus*, Vienna, 1922.
Marx als Denker, Berlin, 1908.
Engels als Denker, 2nd. ed., Berlin, 1925.
Der soziologische Sinne der Lehre von Karl Marx, Leipzig, 1914.
Marxistische Probleme. Beitraege zur Theorie der marxistischen Geschichtsauffassung und Dialektik, 4th ed., Stuttgart, 1919.
Altschul, Eugen: *Die logische Struktur des historischen Materialismus*, Archiv fuer Sozialwissenschaft und Sozialpolitik, Vol. 37.
Barth, Paul: *Philosophie der Geschichte als Soziologie*, 3rd and 4th ed., Leipzig, 1922.
Barth, Theodor: *Der sozialistische Zukunftsstaat*, Berlin, 1879.
Bebel, August: *Aus meinem Leben*, Part II, Stuttgart, 1911.
Bebel, August-Bernstein, Eduard: *Der Briefwechsel zwischen Friedrich Engels und Karl Marx, 1844-1883*, Stuttgart, 1919.
Bernstein, Eduard (ed.): *Die Briefe von Friedrich Engels an Eduard Bernstein, mit Briefen von Karl Kautsky an ebendenselben*, Berlin, 1925.
Bernstein, Eduard: *Probleme des Sozialismus, Neue Zeit*, XXX. Jahrgang, Vol. II, 1912.
Bucharin, N. Ivanovic: *Das Programm der Kommunisten*, Vienna, 1918.
Danneberg, Robert: *Das sozialdemokratische Programm*, 8th ed., Vienna, 1919.
Delbrueck Hans: *Die Marxche Geschichtsphilosophie*, Reclam, 1921.
Diehl, Karl: *Ueber Sozialismus, Kommunismus und Anarchismus*, 2nd enl. ed., Jena, 1911.
Drahn, Ernst: *Friedrich Engels. Ein Lebensbild zu seinem 100 Geburtstage*, Vienna, 1910.
Karl Marx und Friedrich Engels ueber die Diktatur des Proletariats, Berlin, 1920.
Engels, Friedrich: *Ueber die Gewaltstheorie*, Berlin, 1946.
Grundsaetze des Kommunismus. Sozialistische Dokumente, Offenbach, 1947.
Internationales aus dem Volksstaate '1871-1875', Berlin, 1894.
Der Ursprung der Familie, des Privateigentums und des Staates, 9th ed., Stuttgart, 1903.
Die Lage der arbeitenden Klasse in England, 3rd ed., Stuttgart, 1909.
Zur Wohnungsfrage, Singen, 1909.
Ludwig Feuerbach und der Ausgang der Klassischen deutschen Philosophie, Berlin, 1946.
Herrn Eugen Duehrings Umwaelzung der Wissenschaft, 8th ed., Stuttgart, 1914.
Die Entwicklung des Sozialismus von der Utopie zur Wissenschaft, 7th ed., Berlin, 1920.

Zwischen 18 und 25: *Jugendbriefe von Friedrich Engels.* Berlin: Dietz Verlag, 1965.

Ueber den Verfall des Feudalismus u. das Aufkommen der Bourgeoisie, Berlin, 1947.

Fabbri, Firedrich: *Die historischen und sachlichen Zusammenhaenge zwischen Marxismus und Anarchismus*, Archiv fuer Sozilawissenschaften und Sozialpolitik, Vol. XXVI, 1908.

Gerlich, Fritz: *Der Kommunismus als Lehre vom tausendjährigen Reich*, Munich, 1920.

Gray, Alexander: *The Socialist Tradition from Moses to Lenin*, London, 1946.

Gray, J. L.: *Karl Marx and Social Philosophy* in "Social and Political Ideas of the Victorian Age," ed. by F. J. C. Hearnshaw, London, 1933.

Hippel, Ernst von: *Der Bolschewismus*, Duisburg, 1948.

Geschichte der Staatsphilosophie, Meisenheim a. Glau, 1957.

Holstein, Guenther: *Geschichte der Staatsphilosophie*, Munich, 1953.

Kautsky, Karl: *Terrorismus und Kommunismus*, Berlin, 1919.

Friedrich Engels, Sein Leben, sein Wirken, seine Schriften, Berlin, 1895.

Fruehzeit des Marxismus, Briefwechsel Engels-Kautsky (ed. by K. Kautsky) Prag, 1935. Also Berlin, 1908.

Die materialistische Geschichtsauffassung, 2 Vols., Berlin, 1927.

Friedrich Engels' Briefwechsel mit Karl Kautsky, Vienna, 1955.

Die Diktatur des Proletariats, 3rd ed., Vienna, 1918.

Kelsen, Hans: *Sozialismus und Staat*, 2nd ed., Leipzig, 1923.

Vom Wesen und Wert der Demokratie, Tuebingen, 1920.

Lenin, V. Iljitsch: *Selected Works*, translated from the Russian by Marx-Engels-Lenin Institute, Moscow, 12 Vols. 1938.

Staat und Revolution. Die Lehre des Marxismus vom Staat und die Aufgaben des Proletariats in der Revolution. Moscow, 1947.

Lenz, Friedrich: *The Second International*, New York, 1932.

Marx, Karl: *Die Klassenkaempfe in Frankreich 1848-50*, with introduction by Friedrich Engels and a preface by August Bebel, Berlin, 1920.

Selected Correspondence of Marx and Engels (1846-1895), London, 1934.

Selected Works of Marx and Engels, 2 Vols., London, 1942, with annotations thereto in Moscow and London, 1951.

Karl Marx-Friedrich Engels: *Werke*, 36 Vols. Institut fuer Marxismus-Leninismus beim ZK der SED, Berlin, 1961-1964.

Briefwechsel, 4 Vols, Berlin, 1950.

Gesamtausgabe (Mega), Berlin, 1927-1930.

Mautner, Wilhelm: *Bolschewismus und Marxismus. Schmollers Jahrbuch*, 44th issue, Munich and Leipzig, 1920.

Mayer, Gustav: *Friedrich Engels. Eine Biographie*, 2 Vols., Hague, 1934.

Mayer, Siegmund: *Friedrich Engels' Fruehschriften*, Berlin, 1920.

Mehring, Franz: *Aus dem literarischen Nachlass von Karl Marx, Friedrich Engels und Ferdinand Lassalle*, 2nd ed., Stuttgart, 1913.

Die deutsche Sozialdemokratie, Ihre Geschichte und ihre Lehre. 2nd. ed., Bremen, 1878.

Meusel, Alfred: *Die deutsche Revolution von 1848. Mit einem Vorwort von Felix Albini: "Marx und Engels und die Revolution von 1848,"* Berlin, 1948.

Ramm, Thilo: *Die kuenftige Gesellschaftsordnung nach der Theorie von Marx und Engels*, Marxismusstudien, 2nd ed., Tuebingen.

Rosenberg, Arthur: *A History of Bolshevism*, London, 1939.

Sombart, Werner: *Grundlagen und Kritik des Sozialismus*, 2 Vols., Berlin, 1919.

Friedrich Engels, Ein Blatt zur Entwicklungsgeschichte des Sozialismus, Berlin, 1895.

Stepanowa, E. A.: *Friedrich Engels. Sein Leben und Werk*, Berlin, 1958.

Toennis, Ferdinand: *Gemeinschaft und Gesellschaft, Abhandlung des Kommunismus und Sozialismus,* 4th and 5th ed., Berlin, 1922.

Tugen-Baranowsky, Michael, *Theoretische Grundlagen des Marxismus,* Leipzig, 1905.

Woltmann, Ludwig: *Der historische Materialismus,* Duesseldorf, 1900.